TANIA GURDIP SINGH
EARL JASPAL

Foreword by :
Nutan Jain

AF425805

# She is ignificant

## I am Entering my Teens

**First Published in April 2023**

**ISBN: 978-93-5741-285-8**

**E-ISBN : 978-93-5741-582-8**

**BLUEROSE PUBLISHERS**

www.bluerosepublishers.com

info@bluerosepublishers.com

+91 8882 898 898

**Cover Design:**

Yash

**Typographic Design:**

Tanya Raj Upadhyay

Distributed by: BlueRose, Amazon, Flipkart

# I am Entering My Teens

Dedicated to Our Lovely Daughters, Aira and Aizel

# About the Authors

**Dr. Tania Gurdip Singh,** M.S (Obstetrics and Gynaecology) has been working extensively in the field of Obstetrics and Gynaecology for the last fifteen years and is well-known for her analytical approach and great attentiveness and concern towards her patients. She has finished her postgraduation from JNMC, Belgaum, Karnataka, followed by Gynaec Laparoscopy fellowships, Ultrasound trainings and several ART courses. She has published in numerous national and international journals and contributed chapters to several books. Her first book "Clinics in Obstetrics" is a part of National Medical Library, USA. The other books, Ward Round in Obstetrics and Neonatology and Advances in the Management of Obstetric Crisis, are running successfully all over. She is an outstanding medical writer and a teacher par excellence and employing her concepts and perceptions, she has made sincere efforts to simplify this book. This book is dedicated to her patients, past and present.

She is a senior Obstetrician and Gynaecologist and High Risk Pregnancy Specialist working at renowned hospitals in New Delhi, India. Also, she is the Founder and Owner of Safe Mother and Infant Foundation, whose primary aim is to ensure that women receive quality care during pregnancy and child birth and that there should be least NICU admissions.

**Dr. Earl Gaganjot Jaspal**, MD (Pediatrics) has worked as the head of Department of Neonatology at Government Hospital, Ambala, Haryana and has been working in the field of Paediatrics and Neonatology for last fifteen years. He has been awarded certificate of appreciation by Government of Haryana for excellent services in field of Pediatrics and Neonatology. He has finished his post graduation in Pediatrics from Jawaharlal Nehru Medical College, Belgaum, Karnataka and his under graduation from J.S.S Medical College, Mysore, Karnataka. He did his Neonatology training from PGIMER, Chandigarh. He has undergone a Post graduate program in pediatric nutrition, Boston University School of Medicine, USA.

Dr Earl Jaspal has been involved in training activities both at the national and district level. He has been a national Instructor for Facility Based Newborn Care (FBNC) and a regional faculty for many training programs such as Facility Based Integrated Management of Childhood Illness (F-IMNCI), Integrated Management of Childhood Illness (IMNCI), Skilled Birth Attendant ( SBA), Navjat Shishu Suraksha Karyakaram (NSSK) and basic NRP. He has also been a principal investigator of many clinical audits and is a life member of the National Neonatology Forum, Indian Academy of Pediatrics, Indian Medical Association and various other national and international associations.

# Foreword

Dr. Tania has done a great job by bringing out a complete text book, "She is Significant", I am entering my teens. The book is written with young adolescent girls who are entering or have entered their teens, in mind. Now these girls are completely unaware of the physical and mental changes in their bodies once they approach puberty, especially menstruation, vaginal hygiene, fitness, nutrition, etc. At the same time, not only do they undergo a physical transformation, but their mind also changes. Some teens go into depression, some may land up in adolescent pregnancy, and there is no awareness of STDs or birth control methods. Teens may become violent and engage in substance abuse at times. All these topics are discussed in great depth in simple, easy-to-understand language for teens.

Sometimes teenage girls hesitate to talk to their parents about various issues being faced in school or among peers. So this book will be their friend in that instance, explaining the concept of adolescence and helping them traverse this difficult path with ease. The teenage years are a time in life when our children need to be extra careful and vigilant, or else they may land up in great difficulties.

This book will be a boon for parents, especially mothers, as not only the teens but their mothers also have to be very patient in handling their young girls. They should understand that being aggressive towards their children won't help at this stage of life. I highly recommend this book as a must-have for all concerned.

Dr. Nutan Jain M.S. (Obs. & Gynae)
Vardhman Trauma & Laparoscopy Centre Pvt. Ltd
3rd km Jansath Road
Muzaffarnagar-251001 (U.P.) India

# Table of Contents

# Puberty

## Puberty

Puberty is a new normal in a girl's life when she comes out of the world of "Barbie" and "Frozen" and enters a real responsible phase with so many changes in her body. Girls normally start their puberty between 8 to 13 years of age. First the breast buds come under the areola (the small circular area surrounding a nipple) and this new variation is known as thelarche. As puberty progresses, the breast increases in size and there will be changes in its outline and shape. Then, after 1-1.5 years there will be a new change in you, that is, occurrence of hair under the arms and in between the upper thighs, known as pubarche.

Menarche, the onset of menses or periods, arrives approximately 2.5 years after thelarche (0.5-3 years). The average age at that time should be somewhere between 12-13 years. One fine day, you will see bloody spot on your panty. The first look might be scary but you need to get used to it. You need to use sanitary napkins to control the leak which lasts somewhere between 5-7 days.

When all these changes are taking place in your body, all of a sudden you will realize that you are tall!! Yes, there is an increase in height during this time. Arms, legs, hands and feet grow at a faster pace when compared to the rest of the body. Hurray! It's time to buy new clothes and shoes.

Here I would like to talk about a new terminology "Adrenarche". Now adrenarche is an on-going process which takes years to complete. In girls it occurs between 6-20 years of age. It precedes puberty by 2 years and peaks at the age of 20. It is an early stage in sexual maturation and is primarily an emotional and psychological stage of development. Pubarche and adrenarche are sometimes used interchangeably. Over time your face may start looking greasy or oily with spots or bumps on your face, back or may be neck and chest. You will be very tempted to touch or squeeze them but do not do that. It will leave behind bad marks. Hair will often get oily, so need to wash them often. Your breasts will grow bigger; there will be more hair under the arms, on the legs and of course hair between the upper thighs. Armpits will sweat and for the first time, you will notice body odour. There will be mood swings and you might get angry quickly; mommies please don't bother, your daughter is facing the new hormones (oestrogen and progesterone) in her body. Sexual attraction/ sexual desire/ increased libido are other new developments over time.

Slowly the hips will begin to change shape and become wider; waist will get smaller and you will put on weight. But stop stop!! Do not rush to diet. This is absolutely normal.

You may notice white/yellow patches on panty, the vaginal discharge. During puberty, your ovaries will release egg! At times, one breast will be bigger than the other; do not bother at this time. They will even out once they reach their final shape and size. This is the time when you need to wear a bra. Now, you are

GROWN UP! It is time to explore your new identity, learn from your mistakes, share your emotions and be confident to face the world. Yes, this is the new YOU!!

## Precocious Puberty - Tips to prevent

Early onset of puberty (precocious puberty) is when the signs of puberty knocks on your door before 8 years of age (menarche prior to the age of 10), which is quite alarming and is nowadays seen in many girls living in urban areas. On the contrary, some girls belonging to rural areas are still getting their periods at the age of 15 or 16.

Signs of puberty coming earlier do not come alone. They come with more depressive mood swings, much more hormonal imbalances, and stunted growth. There is a blend of psychological and physical discomfort coming the girl's way. The mind and body is not mature enough to handle this change at a small age. This might invite undesirable attention of the opposite sex towards her, which is uncomforting to parents as well. Girls get more conscious about their body and start avoiding social interactions and feel depressed at times. The growth first slows down and once periods begin, growth ceases, thereby affecting the height of the child.

There are many reasons which can be pathological or can be as simple as a sedentary lifestyle and obesity, unhealthy eating habits, feeding your child with more non vegetarian foods treated with hormones and antibiotics, environmental factors, and the list goes endless….

Now what you have to do? Try to eliminate such factors from your child's life, teach them healthy lifestyle which includes exercising on daily basis, yoga, relaxation, avoiding gadgets, eating healthy home-made food and avoiding junk food. You, as parents, should not simply accept early puberty as a trend. Try to approach the doctor for further advice, in order to rule out any related pathology. Even medications can be prescribed to halt puberty if it has come earlier. These medicines will block the production of sex hormones in the body to let the physical changes come at an appropriate time. But let the doctor decide.

### Delayed Puberty

Puberty is said to be delayed if breasts do not develop by age 13 and you do not get your monthly chums by age 16.But important point here is that a girl may achieve all the changes of adrenarche but can still have a delay in puberty. Development of hair in armpits or hair between the legs, acne and body odour are a result of androgen hormones secreted by adrenal glands (located on top of kidneys) in our body. But development of breasts, initiation of periods and other changes occur due to hormones secreted by brain and ovaries. So Girls there is a difference!

Delayed puberty is not always a cause for concern. You may simply be "late bloomer", if someone at home (mother or sister) got it late. Again girls involved in intense exercises or suffering from anorexia nervosa (discussed later in book) experience delayed puberty. Both involve significant reduction in calories, thereby reducing the overall body fat. So leptin (a protein produced by fat cells which triggers your brain to produce hormones) levels decrease in the body and overall production of sex hormones will be hampered. There can be other hormonal imbalances or there can be major issues like structural or genetic abnormalities. If you are on certain medications now or taken radiation therapy in the past for cancer, or you are suffering from anxiety or depression, you can have delayed changes in your body. Consultation with a doctor is a must and the underlying cause needs to be addressed.

# Menarche and Normal Menstrual Cycle

## Overview

The very starting of your monthly flow or shedding of the lining of the womb is called menarche (say "MEN-ar-kee") and when it occurs every month, it is termed a menstrual cycle (which starts from the initiation of one period to the initiation of the next period). The shedding comes in the form of blood which travels from the womb, crossing the mouth of the womb (cervix) through vagina to the outside. You may find it a burden or you may find it friendly (owing to its multiple benefits), the very fact that girls should get periods, will not change. Menses are a part of normal sexual wellbeing for women amidst their reproductive years. It prepares the body for a possible pregnancy. It signifies that you are growing up (attaining puberty) and eventually becoming a lady.

You may call it by any name: Chums, Aunt Flo, Red Wedding, Girl Flu, and as I always say, the list goes on... You may get different feelings, from being low at times to being anxious, angry with mood swings, there might be eruption of pimples, feeling of irritability, during your chums. It is due to a hormonal change going on in your body.

It usually starts sometime between ages 10 and 15. They might start as early as 9 years in few or as late as 16, in some. Every girl's body is different. The menstrual cycle should not be less than 21 days and preferably not more than 35 days. The length might be same or it may vary from cycle to cycle.

Dear girls, periods won't come alone! With them, you will have breast development, hair might appear under your arms and also on the area outside and above your vagina (the fleshy area located just above the top of the vaginal opening is called the mons pubis and so these hair are called pubic hair). Don't be surprised if over the years you see widening of your hips. There might be some clear, stringy liquid coming through vagina (Oh there is a yellowish stain on my panty!!!).



## How will you actually come to know that they are soon arriving?

There is some preparation going on in your body before your periods start. This is nothing but a change in various hormones. Now before you ask me, I will brief you about hormones. Hormones are chemical substances which regulate certain actions in our bodies.

By now, you must be aware of the fact that there are two ovaries in a woman, right and left. Roughly speaking, the ovaries perform two main functions in our bodies; they produce hormones and make female eggs. The most important female hormones released by the ovaries are oestrogen and progesterone. Now, it is these two hormones which play a major role in your menstrual cycle and get your periods.

Your body will give you certain signals that your periods are approaching (as described above). In addition to that, the abdomen might feel bloated, legs start paining, there might be pain in lower back, boobs might feel heavier and tender, and there might be angry or upset moods. You just feel like sitting or even lying down (with knees pulled towards chest). Suddenly, the pain in the lower abdomen increases to some extent and you might see staining of your panty, but this time with a red colour. Pimples are very common in young girls, oh, how they love to appear with your chums (as if these are best friends!).

Menstrual cycle has two main phases. The first phase starts with bleeding and eventually ends up with building the lining of the uterus (the endometrium) and formation of an egg. The second phase prepares the uterus and body to accept a fertilized egg, or to start the next cycle if pregnancy doesn't happen. Towards the end of each menstrual cycle, there is a fall in oestrogen and progesterone hormones, following which menstruation begins, and the whole cycle starts all over again.

Normally, the bleeding phase continues for 5 - 6 days. Initially it is dark brown in colour with less flow, then gets bright red with heavier flow, post which it is lighter and brownish towards the end. Seek a doctor if you see bleeding for less than 2 days, it is scanty in amount or in case it is more than 7 days, the bleeding is heavy or there are clots with it. Bleeding through vagina doesn't mean that you stop your regular day to day activities. Use sanitary napkins (pads) or tampons and change them on regular basis (3-4 times a day), or else this might lead to infection. Some girls prefer a menstrual cup. To use a menstrual cup, a girl inserts it into her vagina. The cup holds the blood until she empties it. If you are careful, no stain will appear on your clothes and no one will come to know that you are bleeding.

Pads have sticky material which sticks on your panty. Tampons are placed inside the vagina. The vagina connects with the uterus, or womb, at the cervix (which means neck). The cervix has strong, thick walls. The opening of the cervix is very small especially in young girls (like a hole), which is why a tampon can never get lost inside a girl's body.

It may take some practice putting in a tampon or menstrual cup, for the first time. Girls going to pool or beach might prefer them. But their use can occasionally cause a girl's hymen to stretch or tear.

The most irritating part of your periods is the pain in your tummy (pain abdomen) especially on day 1 or day 2 of bleeding. Yes, it is horrible! A heating pad, or application of hot water bottle (heat improves blood flow and relieves pain) and pain killers might relieve you of it. Pain killers work well when you take one ahead of the pain. Do not be very regular with pain killers. They have other side effects too! Do exercise on regular basis which will keep a check on your hormones and reduce the intensity of the cramps during periods.

Let me tell you another secret about your ovaries, girls! When a baby girl is born, her ovaries contain a million of eggs, which stay inactive until puberty begins. At the time of puberty, the eggs remain only about 3 lakhs. Towards the end of puberty, girls begin to release eggs as part of their menstrual cycle. But egg is released only once a month, during the middle of your cycle (say day 13 or 14 or 15 of cycle), which marks the second phase of menstrual cycle. It is released in the fallopian tubes (a hollow structure which is the prime location for union of egg and sperm). Tubes are attached to the upper part of the uterus and serve as pathways for the eggs to travel from the ovaries to the uterus.

Girls should get periods each month. But periods might be very irregular during the first couple of years after they start. Be calm! They will be normal in the subsequent years to follow. Don't rush to a doctor until the flow is too heavy to handle or leading to a reduction in your haemoglobin levels.

Well, take periods as your friends, have fun and enjoy life!!

# Premenstrual Syndrome

## What is Premenstrual Syndrome

Knock Knock..... I am coming in a few days! Suddenly you feel bloated with leg cramps and back pain at times, irritability, a sudden change in mood, feel like crying at times, feel weak, heavier breasts, stomach upset, loss of appetite, sex attracts you less, you might be constipated and then you find a tooth that is sweeter than what it usually is......After this follows the phase of bleeding...the PERIODS! This complex of symptoms that occurs 7-10 days before your monthly cycle happens is called premenstrual syndrome. Symptoms often worsen substantially 6 days before, and peak at about 2 days prior to menses, and then eventually the periods begin. Anger and irritability are the most severe complaints and start slightly earlier than other symptoms. Girls should keep an eye on these symptoms before their due date. If they occur continuously every month or for at least 3 consecutive months with a symptom-free interval before ovulation, you can easily label them as premenstrual syndrome (PMS).

PMS occurs due to a decline in sex hormones oestrogen and progesterone and goes away with their surge again, 4-5 days after initiation of monthly bleeding. This can trigger the sebaceous glands to secrete more sebum, an oily substance that lubricates the skin. Too much can result in clogged pores and breakouts and then occurs the most disgusting slice of premenstrual syndrome - PIMPLE, which of course no one likes.

The syndrome occurs in 75% of girls at some point in their lifetime. With age, the symptoms might change in the same person. Symptoms of PMS might worsen in a woman who smoke, take a lot of stress, is sleep and exercise deprived, drink too much alcohol, consume too much refined sugar and red meat. Women who had depression after child birth and who suffer from migraine or asthma are more likely to get PMS. Likewise, family history of depression always plays a role. PMS tends to decline in the decade preceding menopause but in a small segment of females, it deteriorates in the 40s. Girls get absolute relief only once they attain menopause.

Not all girls experience the same symptoms with same severity. In some it may be disturbing but in others its' no BIG deal! At the same time if these symptoms take a harsh turn in the form of depression, sadness, hopelessness, anger, difficulty in concentrating, palpitations leading to disruption of normal daily functioning, the syndrome becomes a premenstrual dysphoric disorder (PMDD). Approximately 8% of women suffer from this disorder which is characterised mainly by severe mood symptoms.

PMS Management

Exercise

Exercise is the first line of management when it comes to PMS. To get the maximum benefit, one should exercise regularly. Research suggests that aerobic exercise can help improve symptoms of PMS, such as depression and fatigue, especially when it is done for one hour thrice a week. Brisk walking, running, biking, and swimming are other good options. There is an increase in endorphins (released from brain) and decrease in adrenal cortisol levels when you exercise. The latter also helps to regulate progesterone and oestrogen synthesis, which in turn helps in reducing the amount of pain and mood swings you get from PMS. Studies recommend a minimum of 30 minutes of aerobic exercise at least 3 days per week to contribute to the regulation of the body composition, mood and to improve physical symptoms. It is also shown that three months of aerobic exercise decreases the PMS complaints significantly.

### Role of Diet in Alleviating PMS Symptoms

Many studies have proven a relationship between PMS and nutrition. Women with PMS have a tendency to consume foods rich in fat and sweet carbohydrates. Overall sugar and caffeine consumption is also high in them. Similarly, intake of high starchy foods has been linked to PMS complaints. In another study comparing healthy, traditional and western diets, it was found that the western diet was more related to PMS than others.

During PMS, protein intake generally lowers down.

A higher complex carbohydrate diet, especially during the late luteal phase, tends to improve mood and reduce food cravings. These foods are thought to help increase the level of serotonin in the brain, which is known to be involved in mood and appetite, premenstrual syndrome subjects may overconsume carbohydrates in an attempt to improve their dysphoric mood state.

A PMS diet including daily intake of whole grains with vitamins, minerals and fibre rich vegetables, fruits and legumes has a positive effect on mood, physical and behavioural symptoms of PMS. Eating plenty of fibre keeps the blood sugar even, which may ease depression, tension, anger, confusion, sadness and further food cravings.

Foods rich in B vitamins may help fight PMS. It is found that women who eat foods high in vitamin B1 i.e. thiamine and vitamin B2 i.e. riboflavin, have significantly lower risk of developing PMS. Taking supplements doesn't give the same effect. Riboflavin, for example, is needed to activate vitamin B6. Taking 100 mg of B6 a day seems to decrease PMS symptoms, especially PMS related depression. B6 helps make "happy neurotransmitters" like serotonin and dopamine. Dopamine regulates motivation, cognition, and pleasure. Serotonin regulates mood, appetite, sleep, memory, and sexual desire. B6 helps make a certain kind of prostaglandin (a type of chemical messenger) that tends to be low in people with PMS. Apart from that B6 regulates hormones, bolsters immune functions, and plays a pivotal role in metabolism. B6 also keeps homocysteine levels in check; without it, too much homocysteine would cause inflammation.

Likewise, thiamine is required to synthesize a neurotransmitter called gamma-amino butyric acid (GABA); low levels of GABA are linked with anxiety.

Clinical trials have also shown that giving women 1,000 to 1,200 mg of supplemental calcium a day for three months significantly improved mood swings, fatigue, pre-menstrual headaches, fluid retention, food cravings and painful cramps. Women with PMS tend to have low levels of calcium at the time of ovulation, which can affect hormones that regulate mood.

Magnesium is yet another useful supplement. Magnesium is involved in the activity of serotonin and other neurotransmitters and plays a role in blood vessel contraction. 300mg of magnesium per day is a good number to start with. Magnesium is particularly supportive when it comes to headaches, fluid retention and mood swings. Magnesium helps balance your 28-day hormone cycle, eases bloating, encourages good sleep, and alleviates anxiety.

DHA (Docosahexaenoic Acid) is an omega-3 fatty acid which is essential for mood-stabilization and to reduce cramps. It aids in decreasing inflammation, and therefore, diminishes menstrual cramps. A study released in 2011 suggests that fish oil may actually be more effective in relieving cramps than ibuprofen.

Vitamin D keeps the entire hormone system stable and balanced. Vitamin D has anti-inflammatory properties and it decreases the production of prostaglandins (a hormone like substance that is responsible for cramps), therefore, a high dose aids in keeping the cramps at bay.

It is notable that gut health is extremely important for overall wellbeing. On-going research shows promising results on the role of probiotics in alleviating stress, anxiety and depression.

Vitamin E (natural alpha-tocopherol) helps in relieving pre-menstrual breast pain and sensitivity. As an antioxidant, it protects breast tissue from inflammation.

Few studies suggest the role of Alpha lipoic acid in the breakdown of excess oestrogen by liver enzymes, which can worsen PMS symptoms if isn't regulated.

*Over the counter drugs can be taken only after consulting a physician.

**Stress Relief and Adequate Sleep**

Because PMS can cause tension, anxiety, and irritability, it's important to find healthy ways to cope with stress. Different strategies work for different women. You may want to try yoga, meditation, massage, writing in a journal, or simply talking with friends. Sleeping for 8 hours at night is a necessity for the proper working of our bodily systems.

## Bright Light Treatment for PMS

Light therapy, whether naturally through the sun, or artificially via the use of a light box, has been shown to reduce feelings of depression, uplifting mood. During light therapy, an individual sits in front of a box that emits bright light that is meant to mimic natural outdoor light. The light hits the hypothalamus which prompts the release of hormones as well as neurotransmitters such as serotonin. Bright Light Therapy during mid-cycle (after ovulation) leads to an improvement in mood particularly in depression, which is hypothesised due to an increased release of serotonin.

# Acne

### Pimples – A General Outlook

Acne vulgaris is the medical name for pimples-- the presence of blackheads, whiteheads, or at times harder, deeper bumps especially on the face. The most common spots for breakouts are the face, neck, chest, upper back, upper arms. Although mild acne may improve with over-the-counter treatments, more severe forms should be treated by a skin specialist.

Acne most commonly affects teenagers, but it is not just a condition of adolescence. Acne is often seen in children as young as 7 years of age. In some cases, acne just marks the beginning of puberty, especially when it occurs even before the development of your boobs or the initiation of your monthly visitors (menses). Likewise, if your parents had suffered with pimples during their adolescence, you have high chances of getting them too!

The exact cause of acne is not known and it is not known why some teens get them while others are more fortunate to go without pimples. In some sense, androgens (male hormones) play a part. Androgens increase in both boys and girls during puberty, making the skin's oil glands get larger with increased production of sebum (lubricates the skin and the hair). Certain medicines can also cause acne. You may get 1-2 bumps, especially around your chums.

Acne in preadolescents is generally milder. When severe acne occurs in this age group, it means that the child will have severe forms in teenage. Getting pimples is not a serious health issue but the problematic part is the permanent scars which it leaves behind.

In few forms of acne, regular skin hygiene may be all that is needed. But your doctor will tell you if you require a step more than that which includes ointments and tablets. In addition, cosmetic treatments can help reduce scarring and changes in skin colour caused by acne.

## Stepwise development of Pimples

When a hair follicle becomes clogged with more and more normal skin cells and on top of that, if it is combined with the oily substance sebum and dead skin cells, it is then called a comedone, which is nothing but a basic acne wound. During adolescence there is additional sebum production, so my dear teenagers are more prone to have one. Eventually, these comedones can develop into mature bumps called whiteheads and blackheads.

## Blackheads

Blackheads are open at the surface of the skin. These are filled with excess oil and dead skin cells. It's not dirt that causes the comedone to turn black. The black hue results from the irregular reflection of light coming from clogged hair follicles. Many a times teens get tempted to squeeze the material out but please do not do that otherwise permanent scars may ensue. Blackheads can frequently be treated with over-the-counter medications.

## Whiteheads

Comedones that stay closed at the surface of the skin are called whiteheads. This happens when oil and skin cells prevent a clogged hair follicle from opening. Many of the same over-the-counter medicines that treat blackheads are also effective against whiteheads.

## Papules or Nodules

These are comedones that become swollen and sore, forming small red or pink bumps on the skin. This type of pimple may be sensitive to touch. Picking or squeezing can make the inflammation worse and may lead to marks and blemishes. When these are pus filled, they are called pustules.

When the inflammation involves the deepest layer of your skin, it forms nodules which, when heal, may leave behind discoloured areas or true scars.

## How should I take care of my skin?

Good skin hygiene is important to support any acne treatment plan. Wash your face no more than twice daily, once in the morning and once in the evening (after returning home). Try not to use hot water for washing. Do not use harsh scrubs or exfoliating products with microbeads, as these can cause irritation to the skin, making acne worse and eventually damaging the skin. Avoid using harsh, deodorant soaps, as well. Instead, use a gentle non-soap facial skin cleanser. Same way, do not scrub the skin with a washcloth or loofah as these can irritate and inflame your acne. Acne does not come from "dirt", so it is not necessary to scrub the skin clean.

In case you intend to use any face wash, consult your doctor for the same. Washes containing salicylic acid or benzoyl peroxide may clear oil from the skin and reduce bacteria, but they may also be drying and can add to irritation.

Try not to "squeeze" or pick your acne, as this can delay healing and may result in scarring or dark spots. Picking can also cause skin infections. Clean ups or facials can better be avoided because any manipulation can lead to more scarring, which increases the likelihood that the skin will not be able to tolerate acne medications.

Wash the skin as soon as possible after playing sports or other activities, which cause a lot of sweating, or coming back after a hectic day.

In case you are using equipment like shoulder pads, helmet straps etc., make sure that these should not make your acne worse.

When you use makeup, moisturizer, or sunscreen, take care that these products are labelled "noncomedogenic", or "won't clog pores", or "won't cause acne". Once you are back home, remove the makeup or any creams on your face gently before snoozing.

Wash or change your pillow case once or twice a week, especially if you use hair products. Try to keep your stress levels under control, which also aggravate acne by increasing the oil production in your skin. Sugary drinks and fried foods can also intensify acne in some. Likewise, constipation should be corrected before seeking treatment for pimples. Eating healthy, home-made food with a lot of greens in your diet goes a long way in preventing acne and giving you that natural glow. Again adequate sleep and hydration are two very essential components when it comes to skin health.

Sometimes, dandruff on the scalp can intensify acne as flakes of dead skin cells on the scalp and hair get transferred to the face and clog the skin pores. So herein lies the importance of washing your scalp and hair on a regular basis.

### Acne Treatment

In moderate to severe cases, you need to consult a skin specialist. Never try to use the same wash, creams or lotions as your friend is using. Your skin is different from hers!! Let the dermatologist read your skin and adjust the medicines and dosages according to your skin type. Please, no over the counter drugs or self-medications!!!!

Medicines for acne try to stop the formation of new pimples by reducing or removing the oil, bacteria, and other things like dead skin cells that clog the pores. They can also decrease the inflammation or irritation response of the skin to bacteria. It may take from 4 to 8 weeks before you see any improvement and know if the medication is effective. Remember, these medications do not "cure" the condition—the acne improves because of the medication. Therefore, treatment must be continued in order to prevent the return of these zits.

There are many types of acne treatments. Some are applied to the skin ("topical" medications) and some are taken by mouth ("oral" medications). In most cases of mild acne, the doctor will start with a topical medication. If acne are more severe and do not respond adequately to a topical medication, or if they cover a large body surface area such as the back and/ or chest, oral antibiotics and/or oral hormone therapy may be prescribed.

# Polycystic Ovarian Syndrome

## An Overview

If talking broadly, PCOS is nothing but a state of hormonal imbalance in which the girls produce an excess of male hormones (much more than they usually make) owing to which they get problems like increased hair growth on the face and elsewhere in the body, pimples, irregular chums, weight gain and many more symptoms. If not treated, it can lead to diabetes (increased sugar in blood), heart problem, high cholesterol levels in blood and may even lead to high blood pressure. The most important of all the consequences is that the ovaries don't make ripe egg and girls have a problem getting pregnant!! The higher amounts of androgens (male hormones) interfere with egg development and release, leading to the absence of ovulation. But that doesn't mean that you cannot get pregnant if you have unprotected intercourse. So, if you're sexually active, use condoms every time you have sex to avoid becoming pregnant or getting a sexually transmitted disease.

Eggs do not mature and instead small fluid filled structures, called cysts, develop in the ovaries. Over a period of time, these cysts become multiple, making the ovaries bigger and heavier. Teens with PCOS are also found to be resistant to insulin (Insulin is a hormone created by your pancreas that controls the amount of glucose in your blood at any given moment).

There is no exact cause of PCOS, but there appears to be some genetic correlation as it tends to run in families.

Adolescence includes critical changes in growth, development and puberty. These changes make the diagnosis of PCOS both challenging and controversial in teens due to the overlap of normal pubertal physiological changes (irregular menstrual cycles, acne and polycystic ovarian morphology on pelvic ultrasound) with adult PCOS diagnostic criteria.

At this point, it is very important to define irregular cycles in adolescents as these are quite different from those occurring in adults. For the very first year post menarche, irregular menstrual cycles are a normal pubertal transition. After the first year but less than 3 years, any cycle which is less than 21 days or occurs after 45 days is considered irregular. If you have passed 3 years post menarche, bleeding occurring in less than 21 days or not occurring for more than 35 days is not normal. Likewise, less than 8 cycles in a year are typical of an irregular menstrual pattern in teens.

Emotional wellbeing is another factor to be discussed when it comes to PCOS in adolescents. Teens get anxious and have depressive moods at times and these changes often go unnoticed and are not recognised. The very physical appearance, which includes obesity, pimples, sometimes hair on the face makes the teen apprehensive and restless. This matter should be looked into with tender loving care as it greatly influences quality of life of the teen. Visit to a psychiatrist is not required at this stage.

**Diagnosis of PCOS**

If your periods are still irregular even after 3 years post initiation, then this needs further evaluation. Periods can be scanty with a gap of 1-2 months or they get heavier. Also features which reflect increased male hormones in young girls, - as in pimples, hair on the face, back, chest and other body parts, increased weight gain, patches of dark, thickened skin on the neck, armpits or between the breasts, should not be ignored. Sometimes you may notice thinning scalp hair. Doctors can perform certain blood tests to learn more about the condition. Ultrasound to look at the ovaries may not be very helpful at this stage of life.

**How will you manage this hormonal Catastrophe?**

Truly speaking, PCOS has no cure, but the best part is that its symptoms can be managed if you make certain alterations to your living pattern.

Lifestyle interventions should lead the list when it comes to hormonal imbalances in the body. This includes a targeted diet, less sedentary behaviour, exercise and behavioural changes. Weight loss is very important in the management of PCOS as it worsens the PCOS symptoms even further. One has to make substantial changes in diet especially eliminating sugar, eating small meals at regular intervals and eliminating fried and junk food. Sometimes professional guidance by a dietician helps you understand healthy food choices. Your doctor may prescribe certain medicines to make your cycles more regular, to reduce pimples and extra hair on the face and body. Each case has to be individualized and given instructions, as all girls with PCOS may not have similar symptoms and may not respond alike with same medicines.

# Unhealthy and Healthy Eating Habits

Although defining a healthy diet is a difficult question to answer, but any diet that eliminates hunger, is safe, reduces all forms of malnutrition, promotes health and is produced without damaging the environment for future generations, is considered a high-quality diet. Of all risk factors, diet is responsible for the largest burden of global ill health and needs immediate and urgent attention. Despite tremendous progress in almost every sphere of life, much of the world does not eat high-quality diets. Health risks are further compounded by easy access to cheap and convenient processed foods, the sedentary lifestyles, engaging in sedentary office jobs, with least indulgence in exercise.

People's leisure time is also being monopolised by passive diversions like television, movies, video games, mobile phones, and other such technologies.

Today we are facing a 'double burden' of under nutrition and being overweight. Low-quality diets are linked to a range of malnutrition and health outcomes, including stunting, wasting, micronutrient deficiencies; overweight and obesity; diet-related, chronic, non-communicable diseases (NCDs); high blood pressure and high cholesterol.

## Changing diets and their impact

Unhealthy diet is known to cause a much deeper impact. Many times, people indulged in eating unhealthy outside food on a regular basis, end up in regretting after consuming these foods. Some people may record physical feelings like feeling bloated, full, sluggish, or sick when describing their possible feelings after consuming junk foods. Finally, they end up feeling ashamed, guilty, regretful, sad and disappointed. Such negative feelings and emotions can lead to anxiety and thoughts of how to compensate - skipping meals, going without something at dinner, performing extra exercise, purging or some other forms of punishment. People should understand that if a healthy, balanced intake of food is practiced for the majority of time, it is healthy and normal to have 'lapses' or enjoy foods solely for the taste or experience e.g. while travelling, family functions, festivals etc. Such small changes need to be embraced as a part of being human.

Likewise, many teenagers are really concerned about their weight and shape. It's not obesity and poor nutrition which worries them; but it is the overemphasis on the importance of being thin and equating thinness with beauty, success and health. Through media exposure, teenagers are also exposed to a number of ways to lose weight and achieve this thin ideal. The net result is that they try to achieve this goal through poor, and sometimes, dangerous nutritional choices. Some teenagers may go in for self-induced emesis, laxative/diuretic or diet pills, for quicker results. It is also found that adolescent girls who are concerned about their weight or who are dieting are more likely to initiate smoking.

Chronic dieting (more than 10 diets in a year), fad dieting, fasting and skipping meals are also classified as unhealthy strategies. Chronic dieting is associated with a variety of symptoms including food preoccupation, distractibility, irritability, fatigue and a tendency to overeat, even binge eat. Not surprisingly, parental criticism of a child's weight, pressure to diet and parental role modelling of dieting are associated with increased dieting rates and increased risk of extreme dieting behaviours. Similarly, people who experience significant psychiatric symptoms, particularly depression and anxiety, are more likely to engage in extreme dieting practices.

## Healthy diet and the right way

Eating healthy is far simpler than one may think. Rather than focusing on what shouldn't be eaten, one should focus on what to eat that will make you healthy and improve your overall health. Foods should be as close to their original form as possible. When food is processed or refined, it's stripped off most of its fibre, vitamins, and minerals, and often preservatives are added in their place. Nowadays, there is a lot of focus on a plant-based diet. But a plant-based diet can be unhealthy too! The following nutritional factors, present in different foods, are a must:

- Omega 3 fatty acids have cardio protective effects

- Folate, vitamin B6 and Vitamin B12 are parts of homocysteine metabolism, and deficiencies of these nutrients result in increased blood levels of homocysteine, which aggravate mental ill health

- Niacin is an effective modulator to increase high-density lipoprotein cholesterol and to improve lipidomic profiles

- Vitamin D lowers the risk of cardiovascular disease and metabolic syndrome

- Antioxidant vitamins (Vitamin A, C, E) are protective against cognitive decline and mental disorders.

There is no single fruit or vegetable that is magical. There is no bad fruit, vegetable, nut, seed, legume, or whole grain. They're all good. Few examples of healthy foods to inculcate in your dietary routine are:

- Fruits: Berries, bananas, citrus, mango, kiwi, apples, melons

- Vegetables: Leafy greens like kale, arugula, and collard greens; peppers; carrots; sweet potatoes; mushroom; squash

- Legumes: Beans, lentils, dried peas, hummus

- Whole grains: Brown rice, wild rice, whole-grain bread, quinoa, amaranth, millet, bulgur

- Nuts and seeds: Almonds, pistachios, cashews, walnuts, chia seeds, flaxseeds, hemp, sunflower, pumpkin seeds.

At least 400 g (five portions) of fruits and vegetables a day should be consumed. Potatoes, sweet potatoes, cassava and other starchy roots are not classified as fruits or vegetables. Limiting intake of free sugars to less than 10% of total energy intake is part of a healthy diet. A further reduction to less than 5% of total energy intake is suggested for additional health benefits. Keeping salt intake to less than 5 g per day helps prevent hypertension and reduces the risk of heart disease and stroke in the adult population.

# Eating Disorders

Eating Disorders (Anorexia Nervosa; Binge Eating; Purging; Bulimia Nervosa) are seen frequently in teenagers. Weight obsession and body image concerns are common among adolescent girls. Eating disorders can cause serious health problems that can become life-threatening.

### Anorexia Nervosa

Anorexia nervosa is an eating disorder wherein the teenager intentionally limits the intake of food in order to lose weight or as a result of fear to gain extra weight. It is not always done by fatter people. Thinner teens do it more often, as they believe that the main gauge of self-worth is their body image. Strict and intense exercise routines are followed in order to maintain the lost weight. Together, this can lead, not only to thinness but to health complications like severe nutritional deficiencies also. Sometimes, the teenager won't realize and can even take it to the extent of serious illness and even death.

Anorexia nervosa often begins with simple dieting. "Innocent" teasing about body weight or appearance, especially by a father, brother or friends may contribute to the onset of anorexia nervosa. It can also be seen in those, pursuing hobbies like modelling, dancing, gymnastics and long distance running where being lean is encouraged. Certain teens always aim to be perfectionists and for them this rule applies to "eating" as well! Soon the weighing scale becomes a close friend. Girls indulge in this behaviour more often as compared to boys.

Once the goal is achieved, they are often under pressure to maintain their hard earned weight. That very pressure or obsession leads to crash dieting resulting in extreme and unhealthy weight loss. There is a reduced intake and increased output of calories. Mostly fats and carbohydrates are targeted and removed from diet. Foods once enjoyed are now refused. They no longer express the desire to eat socially with family or friends.

Once the goal is achieved, the person feels very good and satisfied, is less anxious and has a sense of mastery and accomplishment. Over time, the various nutritional deficiencies start causing problems of their own that may increase anxiety, stress and negative mood.

Now, anorexia nervosa can be divided into two subgroups:

One is where the intake of food is severely limited through dieting or fasting, together with intense workouts to lose and then maintain that lost weight.

Second is bulimia, wherein the adolescent eats large amounts of food in a brief period of time (binge eating) and then gets rid of the eaten food by intentionally vomiting, misusing laxatives, enemas or even taking diuretics. This habit of getting rid of the food eaten (purging) is followed on a regular basis as they can't control their urge to eat large amounts of food. People who have a binge eating disorder are often embarrassed by the amount of food they eat. They may hide and binge in private. Binge eating makes them fat. So, they find ways to take it out and indulge in purging which makes them suddenly disappear after eating food. Bulimia patients can take other steps like excessive exercising or fasting to get a slender body. Bulimia often starts in the late teens. Depression can be one cause of bulimia. Once bulimia is practised consistently, an adolescent ends up with a nutritional deficiency, eventually leading to anorexia nervosa.

Anorexia can be fatal. It can affect any organ system in the body. Many teens with the disorder initially keep their illness very private and hidden. Still, it can be diagnosed once a clear history is taken. Intense dieting with a strong fear of gaining weight and a distorted body shape and size is the clue. Many girls even have missed periods. The person tends to hide or discard the food, would be counting calories often before eating food, and would deny that they are hungry. They often lack energy, feel tired, cold and weak. With very little intake of food, constipation sets in. There can be slower heart beat and fainting attacks. Complain of hair loss and skin dryness become frequent. Dental cavities, erosion of tooth enamel, and a change in nail quality can be seen. Headaches and loss of muscle mass are often noted. Teens are socially withdrawn, irritable and moody and are most of the times seen depressed. They may become overly sensitive to criticism. Infections get more common. Dehydration can result in dark coloured urine. These teens are at increased risk for fractures. Low haemoglobin is common.

Why do some teens develop anorexia nervosa and others do not? Well, there is no one cause of an eating disorder. A constant desire for a thin body drives this disorder. Family relationships, psychological problems and genetics, are all linked to it. Each case has to be evaluated individually. Adolescents with anorexia nervosa are often resistant to treatment and think that their weight is normal. Support from family, friends and teachers is crucial. Medical care is based on nutritional rehabilitation and behaviour modification, together with psychological treatment. Once nutritional deficiency is fulfilled, mood will be elevated on its own. Moreover, having healthy adult role models who do not talk about body shape or size, dieting, fat, or losing weight, is helpful.

One has to be really careful as anorexia nervosa can relapse. Anorexia nervosa for a longer duration can lead to many long- term adverse effects.

# Nutrition and micronutrient deficiencies in Teenage

*Why is Nutrition so important in Adolescents?*

Adolescence is a state of rapid physical and mental growth. Dietary habits established in adolescence can have a long lasting effect on adult health. This is a period of constant nutrient demand. Overall development of a teen is very much dependent upon nutritional requirements - including those for energy, protein, iron, calcium, and others. Suboptimal nutrition can lead to anaemia, stunted growth, being underweight, there can be a delay in attaining puberty, and it can also hamper the cognitive growth. Poor nutrition is more common among rural areas and in large families with uneducated parents. Unhealthy eating habits contribute to these deficiencies to a large extent.

### Common Nutritional Deficiencies in Teens

One of the most important nutrient deficiencies in teens is iron deficiency. **Iron** helps move oxygen from the lungs to the rest of the body and helps muscles store and use oxygen. If your diet lacks iron, you might develop a condition called iron deficiency. Adolescent girls are also at higher risk of iron deficiency because their bodies lose iron during menses.

In case you get tired too soon, your skin is getting paler day by day, you don't feel like eating anything at times or skipping your meals, you get abnormal rapid breathing while walking, climbing, or playing, please check your haemoglobin and iron stores in the body. Often, you can experience cold hands and feet, frequent infections or an unusual craving for non-nutritious substances like chalk, paint, ice, dirt or starch.

There are two types of iron in foods, i.e. heme iron and non-heme iron. Heme iron is derived primarily from animal sources such as meat, poultry and fish. Non-heme iron is found in plant sources such as dark leafy vegetables, cereals and beans. Try to include iron rich foods as part of your healthy diet. Vitamin C helps promote the absorption of iron in the diet, so include vitamin C rich foods such as citrus fruits, cantaloupe, strawberries, bell peppers, tomatoes and dark green vegetables.

If I talk about bones, what will first come to your mind— yes, definitely **calcium**, as our bones have body's 99% of calcium. Again, it is very important for teeth, blood clotting, for our heart and nerves. Calcium needs are greater during puberty and adolescence. The body acquires its calcium needs from two sources. Calcium rich foods or a supplement are one way to get it. In case our diet is deficient in calcium, the body will obtain its requirement of calcium by removing it from our bones. So, in that case you have weaker bones!!! Herein lies the reason why your mom is always asking you to consume dairy products, nuts, green vegetables and fruits - all give you calcium.

Zinc is yet another very important trace element our body always looks for! Zinc is known to be a heavy hitter when it comes to growth of our cells, in protein building in our body, creation of our genetic material and a key player in maintaining a healthy immune system. It refines the senses of smell and taste. More than 300 enzymes in the body require zinc for their production. So, zinc is that very important. Meat, poultry and seafood are rich in zinc. Dairy products, whole grains and legumes also contain zinc. Consuming too much zinc can interfere with the absorption of iron and copper and even causes nausea and vomiting.

Do you actually know what **vitamin D** is? No, you do not! Technically, vitamin D is a misnomer. It is a hormone!! It is not a true vitamin because it can be produced in the body in response to sunlight exposure of the skin, hence its name "the sunshine vitamin". Only 10% of the vitamin D in the body comes through our diet. In the body, vitamin D is converted into calcitriol, an active form, by the liver and kidneys. This in turn helps absorb calcium from food and prevents calcium loss from the kidneys. So before taking calcium, think of vitamin D which is extremely important for retaining that calcium in your body, thereby maintaining bone health. It is seen that vitamin D has a role in reducing cancer growth in the body; it helps fight infections, fatigue, muscle weakness, development of diabetes and helps in preserving heart health. Oily fish is a good source of this vitamin. But it is always better to take supplements when it comes to vitamin D as its requirement is never completely fulfilled by diet alone.

**Vitamin B12**, also known as cobalamin, is another significant vitamin which is found mostly in animal foods. Vegetarian diets are low in this vitamin. Proper functioning of the brain, formation of red blood cells in the body and formation of genetic material- DNA, are few of the vital functions of vitamin B12. If you are experiencing numbness, tingling, memory loss, depression and muscle weakness - first thing that should come to your mind is low vitamin B12 levels (but better get it checked before starting any supplements). Again, constipation, diarrhoea, loss of appetite, gas, bloating can be triggered by a vitamin B12 deficiency. There are a variety of vitamin B12 supplements available. Fish, shellfish, liver, red meat, eggs and dairy products are rich sources of vitamin B12.

**Folate** (Folic acid) - Vitamin B9 helps in the production of genetic material DNA and RNA in the body. Metabolism of protein is also dependent on it. Vitamin B9 and Vitamin B12 go hand in hand to help make red blood cells and help iron work properly in the body. Tissue growth and cell function is reliant on folate. So, this vitamin is very essential for teens. It plays a key role in breaking down homocysteine, an amino acid that can exert harmful effects in the body if it is present in high amounts. Rich sources of folate are dark green leafy vegetables, legumes, nuts, sunflower seeds, egg, to name a few.

**Iodine**- Again a very essential mineral which is required in traces in the body. In order to make thyroid hormones in the body, iodine is indispensable. Thyroid hormones control many functions in the body, including growth and development. Because our body does not produce iodine, it has to be supplemented in the diet. Without enough iodine, thyroid hormones do not work properly and can lead to underactive or overactive thyroid gland. If you are eating a healthy and balanced diet, extra iodine supplements may not be required. Lack of iodine in the body can be reflected as a swelling of thyroid gland, a visible lump (goitre) on your neck. There can be weight gain, fatigue and weakness. Thinning of hair, dry skin, slower heart rate, feeling colder than usual and learning and memory difficulties are all its adverse effects. Iodized table salt is the easiest way to fulfil the daily iodine requirement. Sources of iodine in the diet are dairy products, seafood, seaweed (kelp), eggs and some vegetables.

**Vitamin** A- Although required in small amounts, this vitamin is very essential for the normal functioning of the visual system. This is again a significant contributor to cell growth, production of red blood cells and plays a pivotal role in overall immunity. To maintain the reproductive health of the teen, participation of vitamin A is necessary. The human diet contains two sources for vitamin A: preformed vitamin A (retinol and retinyl esters) and provitamin A carotenoids. Preformed vitamin A is found in foods from animal sources, including dairy products, eggs, fish, and organ meats. Provitamin A carotenoids are obtained from plant-based foods, which are then converted into vitamin A in the intestine. The main provitamin A carotenoids in the human diet are beta-carotene, alpha-carotene, and beta-cryptoxanthin. Most vitamin A is stored in the liver. If you have to measure vitamin A in the body, retinol levels have to be checked.

# Being Overweight and Weight Loss Strategies

## Understanding Weight Gain Pattern in Teens

A child is different from a teen when it comes to weight gain. Children are generally short with chubby cheeks and a plump look, which means height increases later. But the pattern is reversed in teens, wherein the height grows before gaining weight. In teen girls, peak height growth occurs between ages 11-13 years. In boys, the peak height gain happens between 13 and 15 years, on an average. Girls can gain 15 pounds (6-7 kg) whereas boys generally gain double the weight, approximately 30 pounds (13-14 kg). Anything more than that is not good until or unless there is a family history of obesity and especially when it is the result of unhealthy eating habits and being inactive most of the day. On an average, girls gain more fat than boys.

## What actually leads to Obesity?

Teens are given more liberty and freedom, as compared to children; to move around with friends, party, go for a movie and so many other things. There is a kind of habit in each family of giving pocket money to children once they enter their teens. That is where they indulge in eating more of junk and fried food. That's a tender age when they relish these foods and are either unable to differentiate between hygienic and unhygienic foods or simply, they overlook this fact. These diets are high in calories without any nutrition.

There is somehow reduced physical activity in teens due to study pressure, clearing exams, sitting for long hours and of course, when you study more, u require more energy and invariably you land up eating more. Packed foods late at night are the real contributors! If there is unexplained weight gain, seek a doctor's advice as it can be a medical problem your teen is facing. In such a situation, don't pressurize your teen to exercise more or comment on her appearance. This may lower her self-esteem when, actually, she is not at fault.

## Risks of being Overweight and Obese

There can be an increased risk of high blood pressure, heart problems and diabetes. If you are carrying more weight, you tend to have breathing difficulties; it may trouble your sleep and cause you to snore while sleeping! Extra weight puts a lot of strain on your joints. Hormones in your blood will change, producing undesired results. Emotionally, the teen becomes weak, with low self-confidence making them less popular with their peers. The child is often depressed, anxious, and not keen to take part in various activities. Obsessive compulsive disorder can also occur.

## What is to be done?

Restrictive and fancy diets are not for teens. This is their growing age; their body needs certain vitamins and nutrients so that all bodily systems function normally. There will be other health issues which will crop up. The same is not going to end here; the teens will be subjected to long term mental and physical problems. Healthy eating habits and lifestyle modifications should lead the drive. If your child is dissatisfied with your choices, a nutritionist help can be sought for, instead of simply sitting and giving inspirational lectures.

First and foremost is to modify the environment at home. If parents indulge in eating junk food, using extra oil at home, eating too much at a time, not following a physical fitness regime or in short, are not disciplined when it comes to health, then you cannot expect the opposite from your child. Most children do what they see at home. So, change the atmosphere at home. Lead by example; show your teen what it actually means. When a teen has overweight parents, it's often very difficult for that teen to lose weight.

Getting packaged and frozen foods, which contains a high amount of salt and preservatives, should be completely discarded. Because teens are growing rapidly, they have a voracious appetite and will often eat what's available to them. Healthy options can be yogurt, nuts, fresh fruits, seeds, popcorns, or any food which can be prepared at home.

Timing the meals and portioning the food is another significant aspect. Eating small meals at 2-3 hourly intervals pay in the long run. Bloating, acidity and many stomach ailments start only when there are long gaps in between your meals. Do not skip your meals. Usually, you feel hungrier at the next meal and over-eat the rest of the day. Skipping meals changes your metabolism, which makes it even easier to gain weight. Being hungry can have a negative impact on a teen's concentration and education.

Teens are totally heedless of the concept of adequate hydration. The habit of drinking sufficient water should be inculcated from the very beginning. Every cell of the body is dependent on water for its functions. It maintains body temperature, lubricates our joints, removes waste from the body, and helps the body in so many other ways. Teens should drink somewhere between 6-8 glasses of water every day. Tea, coffee, milk, juices and other packaged drinks cannot substitute water.

One of the very good indicators of enough water intake is the colour of the urine. If hydration is adequate, urine will be pale yellow or colourless. In case the water intake is not sufficient, the colour of the urine turns dark yellow or amber coloured. Also, physical activity of adolescents is more; some are indulged in playing various sports, others love gymming, this gives more reason that water level in their body should be balanced.

Switch off all gadgets when your child is eating. This way, they tend to overeat. They simply forget to pay attention to how much they are eating. Limiting distractions while eating go a long way. Make them eat slowly and gradually, which helps them consume a lesser quantity of food. Eating mindfully generates decent outcomes.

Protein rich foods should be added to the diet or as snacks, because they give a feeling of fullness for a long time. So, your child will not be disturbed by hunger cravings.

Talk to your child when they are sad, stressed or tired. Stress is a major contributor to overeating. Exercising, yoga, meditation, all relieve stress. Let your child choose her favourite physical activity. They will utilize their time, eat less and have less stress.

Tracking the diet is another step towards achieving your goal of fitness. A good practice would be to maintain a small diary and jot down all the dietary things you consume. This awareness may help you stick to your dietary plan.

Retaining a timely sleep everyday really helps shed those extra kilos. Ghrelin and leptin are two hormones which go hand in hand in balancing sleep and appetite. When you are sleep deprived, you have less leptin and more ghrelin. Leptin will tell you when to stop eating and ghrelin, on the other hand, tells you when to eat. This equation between these hormones should be balanced by 7-8 hours of sound sleep.

Spend time with your teen. Go together for a walk, to the gym, to the grocery store or just watch a movie together. This bonding with the teen gives you time to encourage them so that they stay motivated in their aim. You can change their mind and make them do certain things which they feel are not possible for them. Help them set small, manageable goals in the beginning of their journey. Sometimes weight loss is not evident in the first few days or weeks. Speak to them about the importance of inch loss, which they may not have heard before. Standing on the weighing scale everyday will not give you any additional benefits. Check your weight once in fortnight.

Take the stairs when you can, walk or at least stand whenever you get the opportunity. You can move your body parts while standing, which is another form of physical activity. Help your mom at home in household chores or at least do your work yourself.

Keep your mind diverted by indulging in useful activities as 'boredom eating' is harmful. Limit sugar intake, even at home. Cut down unhealthy fats, rather than completely eliminating fats from one's diet.

# Fitness in Teens

## What Fitness means in Teens!

If you want to be healthy, you have to be fit. But does fitness always mean hitting the gym? The answer is No, especially in your early teens. It is advised that working out at the gym is good after 14 years of age, as puberty strikes and natural growth is over by then. It is not healthy for children to exercise especially at the gym. They should take up a sport. Wrong exercises can deform their soft and supple bones. Lifting weights might even stunt their height. Even if children join gyms, they should only do cardio and freehand exercises. They should never be left unsupervised.

You don't always have to lift weights to make your muscles and bones stronger. American

*Academy of Paediatrics recommends the following physical activities for teens which help in muscle as well as bone strengthening:*

- Washing and waxing a car for 45 to 60 minutes

- Washing windows or floors for 45 to 60 minutes

- Playing volleyball for 45 minutes

- Playing touch football for 30 to 45 minutes

- Gardening for 30 to 45 minutes

- Shooting baskets for 30 minutes

- Bicycling 5 miles in 30 minutes

- Dancing fast for 30 minutes

- Raking leaves for 30 minutes

- Walking 2 miles in 30 minutes

- Performing water aerobics for 30 minutes

- Swimming laps for 20 minutes

- Playing a game of basketball for 15 to 20 minutes

- Bicycling 4 miles in 15 minutes

- Jumping rope for 15 minutes

- Running 1 1/2 miles in 15 minutes

- Shovelling snow for 15 minutes

- Stair climbing for 15 minutes

Apart from the above mentioned exercises, roller skating, hiking, soccer, tag games, and, skiing, can be other examples. Yoga, aerobics and pilates are further ways to relieve the stress of studies, homework and the fear of competitions. The teen can choose anything from the above or a combination of two activities, depending on his/her calibre and stamina. Exercise is very important for the overall growth of the adolescent. Daily exercise may help prevent conditions such as weight gain, high blood pressure, type 2 diabetes, abnormal cholesterol levels, heart problems and other such ailments later in life. Anything between 45-60 minutes per day for 5 days a week is considered fine. Encouraging healthy lifestyles in children and teens is very important for their future as adults, as it is largely going to affect them as they grow up. Inculcate the fitness mantra in your child from the very beginning because certain habits are difficult to adopt once you grow up. For this to become a reality, the whole family should get involved. Lead by example because the child very quickly adopts what his/her parents follow.

Exercising regularly helps the teen in several ways. From improving the blood circulation in the body, to keeping body weight under control, preventing bone loss, building muscles, helping manage stress and improving self-image, the list of benefits goes endless. Brain health and overall learning are empowered. Sleep becomes better and sound. Following any sport on regular basis gives you a sense of accomplishment because you are learning something new every day, away from your monotonous regime. Being fit from the very teenage helps you age well later when you grow up. Like the fruit doesn't get ripe in one day, so the benefits will be known as the age advances. Especially girls will be away from the hormonal disturbances which are very common in teens. Exercise can also help the body stay flexible, and your muscles and joints will stretch and bend easily.

When the exercise becomes boring, it is then when you find the majority of dropouts. You lose interest when you do the same thing again and again. So, friends, make your exercise adventurous and fun filled by adding a variety to it. Try different sports and different activities and see which motivates you the most. Always take a break in between for a day or two to rejuvenate your inner self and bounce back with new energy. Even if you are suffering from any medical disorder, try to move more and sit less. Approach an expert and try to look for exercise which suits your health condition. Remember, it's never too late to start exercising.

# Human Papilloma Virus Vaccination

## *Understanding the need of HPV Vaccination*

Cervix (neck of the uterus) is the lower portion of the uterus, which connects the vagina with the main body of the uterus. Cancer of the cervix is the fourth most common cancer among women in the world. Many factors contribute to the development of this fatal disease, such as socio-economic status, sexual intercourse, immune compromised state, habits like smoking and alcohol consumption, to name a few. However, the most important factor that has a huge impact on the development of cervical cancer is primarily persistent infection with human papilloma virus. Mainly 4 types of human papilloma virus cause cancer of the cervix: Type 16 causes cancer in 60% of cases, type 18 in 18% of cases, type 45 in 8% and 5% of infection is caused by HPV31.

Human papilloma virus is extremely common worldwide having more than 100 types, out of which at least 14 are cancer-causing. HPV is mainly transmitted through sexual contact, wherein penetrative sex is not mandatory for transmission. Even skin-to-skin contact is enough for transmission. Most individuals contract the disease shortly after the onset of sexual activity, which makes it one of the most frequently spread viruses in the world.

In 90% of cases, HPV gets completely cleared from the body within the first couple of years after contracting the infection, if the host has good immunity. In most of the infected cases, symptoms are generally absent, which makes people reluctant to take any screening tests to determine the absence or presence of disease, even if they are already infected. In few cases, infection becomes persistent and virus remains for years, eventually leading to cancers or warts depending upon the virus strain. It takes 15 to 20 years for cervical cancer to develop in women with normal immune systems. It can take only 5 to 10 years in women with weakened immune systems, such as those with untreated HIV infection.

Women most often get infected with the virus between 15 and 25 years of age. In both genders, the risk of HPV infection is around 50% throughout life. HPV can, not only cause cervical cancer, but certain HPV types can cause cancers of the anus, vulva (the visible external female genitalia), vagina, penis and oropharynx (part of the throat at the back of the mouth).

Certain HPV types (6 and 11) can cause genital warts and respiratory papillomatosis (a disease in which tumours grow in the air passages leading from the nose and mouth into the lungs). Genital warts are very common, highly infectious and affect sexual life.

## HPV Prevention with Vaccination

Primary prevention in the form of HPV vaccination is the first and foremost step in the management of cervical cancer, which can be cured, if diagnosed at an early stage and treated promptly. Cancer of other body parts (mentioned above) is also preventable using similar primary prevention strategies. When a person is given this vaccine, the immune system (the body's natural defence system) will make antibodies against HPV. These antibodies are expected to protect against disease caused by HPV. But at the same time, vaccine does not eliminate the necessity for vaccine recipients to undergo screening for these infections. Vaccines may not demonstrate protection in cases where the person is already infected with the virus. Also, vaccines are not a treatment for any cancer; they are used only for prevention.

The first approved vaccine was a quadrivalent formulation called Gardasil, now replaced with the newest generation Gardasil 9 (9-valent HVP vaccine), both of which are highly efficacious in preventing cervical cancer.

GARDASIL 9 is indicated in females 9 through 45 years of age for the prevention of cervical, vulvar, vaginal, anal, oropharyngeal and other head and neck cancers caused by human papillomavirus (HPV) Types 16, 18, 31, 33, 45, 52, and 58; cervical, vulvar, vaginal, and anal precancerous or dysplastic lesions caused by HPV Types 6, 11, 16, 18, 31, 33, 45,

52, and 58; and genital warts caused by HPV Types 6 and 11.

GARDASIL 9 is indicated in males 9 through 45 years of age for the prevention of anal, oropharyngeal and other head and neck cancers caused by HPV Types 16, 18, 31, 33, 45, 52, and 58; anal precancerous or dysplastic lesions caused by HPV Types 6, 11, 16, 18, 31, 33, 45, 52, and 58; and genital warts caused by HPV Types 6 and 11.

Cervarix is another vaccine on the market (bivalent vaccine against HPV 16 and 18 infections), which is recommended to vaccinate adolescent girls (10-14 years).

Before 14 years of age, generally 2 doses are adequate. From 15 years onwards, 3 doses are recommended. Administration at a tender age becomes important so that young boys and girls receive protection before they get sexually active and before they are ready to begin routine cytological and other molecular tests. Other facts about the dose, route of administration and safety profile of the vaccine can be talked with your physician administering the vaccine.

Vaccines, like any other medicine, can have side effects. Many people who get the HPV vaccine have no side effects at all. The most common side effects of HPV vaccine are usually mild and include:

- Pain, redness, or swelling in the arm where the shot was given

- Fever

- Headache or feeling tired

- Nausea

- Muscle or joint pain

On very rare occasions, severe (anaphylactic) allergic reactions may occur after vaccination.

# Douching

## What Is Douching?

The word "douche", in French, means "wash" or "soak." It is a method to clean the inside of the vagina, but, yes, not with soap and water. A douche is a pre-packaged fluid mixture that may contain antiseptics and fragrances. Or simply, it can be a mixture of water and vinegar. A douche comes in a bottle or bag and is sprayed through a tube or other tool upward into the vagina.

## To Douche or Not to Douche - Let's understand the basics!

Generally, we all as girls feel that our vagina should be clean and above all odours free. May be somewhere it is inculcated in our culture, maybe we have seen or heard it at home or read it somewhere or maybe our inner sense tells us to do so. But modern medical practice has a different school of thought. They somehow do not find any good in doing that. Their reasoning is somewhat valid, I personally feel.

You know different parts of your body have their own pH balances, including your vagina, which should be maintained at all times to keep it infection free. Now let us first understand what is pH. The pH measures the acidity of any substance. It ranges from 0 to 14, with 0 being the most acidic, 7 being neutral, and 14 being the most basic (alkaline). Now the vagina has a pH between 3.8 and 4.5, so it is acidic. If the pH of the vagina increases (it gets less acidic), the quality or amount of lactobacilli (friendly bacteria which should be present in the vagina) can fall and other bad bacteria can multiply.

Now there has to be a certain amount of vaginal discharge to keep it lubricated. The discharge or secretions comes from glands in your vagina and cervix (mouth of the uterus). This fluid also contains lactobacilli, the normal bacterial flora of the vagina. After the bowel, the vagina has the largest number of healthy bacteria in the body and they are there for a reason.

The discharge or fluid flows out of the vagina each day, cleansing old cells and debris that have lined the vagina. This is completely a natural process—it's your body's way of keeping your vagina healthy and clean. At the same time, it maintains the pH of vagina. Therefore, what is important is to maintain this delicate balance of bacteria to keep your pH levels ideal and have proper moisture in the vagina. Normal vaginal discharge is usually clear or little milky.

Remember that vagina has a natural odour, a subtle scent that is not unpleasant or foul smelling (Vaginas aren't meant to smell like flowers!!) Washing out your vagina doesn't get rid of odour (odour that is typically normal and healthy for women), and can increase your risk of vaginal dryness, irritation, and infection.

The colour, consistency, and amount of discharge keep on changing and are different in different phases of your menstrual cycle. Its' simply one way of telling which phase of your menstrual cycle you're in. These are purely hormonal changes.

When periods begin, the discharge is red in colour, of course because you are menstruating (shedding the lining of the uterus). Immediately after periods, most of us will not notice any cervical fluid for a couple of days. Roughly from day 8th to day 13th of your cycle, you may experience more fluid which is thick or sticky and become wetter and creamier. It may look whitish and cloudy, or even yellowish (especially when it gets dry on your underwear). As ovulation approaches, much more fluid is produced. Your vagina will likely start to feel much wetter, and fluid will become more slippery as its water content rises. It becomes more stretchy and clearer. Just prior to ovulation, the discharge often resembles a raw egg white that you can stretch for inches between your thumb and finger. Once ovulation is over, the fluid amount again decreases.

What I mean to say is that every human body is unique - these changes may show up differently for you, or you may experience or interpret them in a different way. But young girls, please try to learn about your body!!

### So, now, what should be done instead?

The best answer to this is to actually do nothing. Leave your vagina alone. Do not douche. Douching can take out everything that's in your vagina. This process can raise the vaginal pH and such changes make the environment more favourable for the growth of bacteria that cause infection. Let your vagina be self-sufficient to do its job of self-cleaning. Simply, wash the area around your vagina with soap and water. Do not try to wash the inside of the vagina. At times soap can also increase the vaginal pH and can disturb the natural bacteria levels. So, try a cleanser specifically designed to maintain the pH of the vagina. During your periods, washing more than once a day may be helpful as there is a need to keep the area between the vagina and anus clean.

Put down those deodorants, perfumes, sprays or scented wipes. Do not get embarrassed by the odour down there. Do not think that douching will make you cleaner. Instead, you are doing more harm to your vagina. Sometimes, the ingredients of a douche may cause an allergic reaction. Also, there's no evidence that douching protects against sexually transmitted diseases or vaginal infections, on the other hand, it may even increase the risk.

Douching can even lead to problems getting pregnant. Vaginal dryness is another issue with douching as it removes or alters the natural mucous of the vaginal walls.

Now, you will ask me, "Can I douche with water alone? My answer to this would be to just stay away from it. Still if you really feel the need, then, yes, water is at least better than the other douching agents available in the market.

## Let your vagina breathe

Wear breathable cotton underwear and ditch the nylon, satin or silk panties all together. The panties should not be tight fitted. They restrict the airflow and encourage bacteria to grow. Also try to remove the underwear especially when you sleep.

It is important to keep the vagina dry and the surrounding area clean to avoid excess moisture.

## Build Immunity

Take care of your immune health. A balanced, nutritious diet with plenty of oral fluids is the key to maintain your vaginal and reproductive health. Yogurt or simply curd intake should be a daily routine. These are rich in probiotics. Probiotics are live bacteria and yeasts that are good for you, especially your digestive system. The live bacteria found in yogurt are lactobacillus acidophilus and these are the ones which are naturally found in the vagina.

Maintaining an overall wellbeing by exercising regularly, avoiding junk food and excess sugar, drinking adequate water, indulging in creative and mindful hobbies, and getting an adequate sleep are ways to support a balanced vaginal health. Smoking and drinking have a poor impact on your vaginal health. Say goodbye to all such habits.

## Not all odours are good!

A persistent and foul odour, or any odour accompanied by a thick or greenish discharge, is a wakeup call. Again, itching, soreness, irritation, a burning sensation, and rawness in the vaginal area makes it compulsory to seek medical advice. These can be signs of serious vaginal infections. In that case, the doctor may prescribe certain medications, probiotics and even a vaginal wash. These infections are easily treatable.

### Safe Sex

Protect your vagina against bad infections like chlamydia, gonorrhoea, genital herpes, genital warts, syphilis and HIV by using condoms every time you have sex. Certain lubricants can be used to lubricate the vagina but do not use petroleum jelly. If you're using condoms for protection, do not use an oil-based lubricant - they can cause the latex in condoms to break down. Using condoms eliminates the need for douching (certain women want to get rid of male secretions by douching, forgetting that douching is not a valid form of contraception!).

### Hygiene

After a bowel movement, wipe from front to back to avoid bacterial contamination of the vagina.

### Use of panty liners

Another option is to wear a panty liner. These are nothing but a much smaller and thinner form of sanitary napkins. Panty liner keeps your inner wear dry. These are meant to be used on non-period days to absorb the vaginal discharge. But girls, please do change them often (minimum three-four times daily).

# Sexually Transmitted Diseases in Teens

## Overview

As the name suggests, sexually transmitted diseases (STIs) spread through sex (vaginal, anal or oral). Sometimes they can spread through close contact with the genitals or body fluids. STIs are common among teens. If you are sexually active, you should be fully aware of the diseases you can contract, what are the symptoms, how they look, what is the treatment and whom to approach. People who had a STI before are more prone to get it again. Many diseases like HIV/AIDS remain with you lifelong, so be extra careful. The best way to protect yourself from STIs is either to not have sex or use protection (condoms)

EVERYTIME you have sex. It is always better to have intercourse with only one partner at a time. When in doubt, get the partner tested before having any intimate relationships. Make it a point to get checked and tested at least once a year especially if you are not using condoms or you are having multiple sexual partners. Only have sex with a partner who does not have sex with anyone else.

Many teens are actually hesitant to talk openly and honestly with a doctor or nurse about their sex lives. You need to understand that girls' bodies are biologically more prone to get sexually transmitted diseases, so please talk and express if you have a sexual partner or partners. Talk to the doctor about vaccines against HPV and hepatitis B. Once you start the treatment of any STI, finish it till the end. DO NOT leave in between once you start feeling better, the infection may not be completely over!

Well let me give you some idea about the various sexually transmitted diseases:

### Chlamydia and Gonorrhoea

There are no symptoms so you get them easily from having sex with someone who is already infected. If at all you get symptoms, these can come in the form of discharge from the vagina, anus and can be associated with fever, pain in lower belly, or pain while you pee. You can have bleeding between periods or bleeding after intercourse. Pain during sex is not uncommon. But both the infections are curable with antibiotics. Get repeat testing 3 months after getting treated. Partner should be treated as well. Do not have intercourse till the infection completely goes. If left untreated, girls can have pelvic inflammation and their fallopian tubes can get blocked leading to trouble in conceiving later in life. Pelvic inflammation causes really bad pain in the lower belly, sometimes radiating to the back. There can be infection in the blood that can lead to problems in various joints in your body.

## Genital Herpes

Like chlamydia and gonorrhoea, genital herpes does not present with any symptoms. But unlike them, genital herpes has no cure, you can get treated and control the infection. In some teens, there can be presence of blisters or sores on the sexual organs that are outside of their body, which when treated go away in a few weeks. The blisters tend to come more when you are in stress, getting anxious, tired, not feeling well, in sunlight or during periods. There are two variants of the virus: HSV 1 (mainly causes cold sores around mouth; can lead to genital herpes only when oral sex was done) and HSV 2 (most of the time this is the causing factor of genital herpes). Presence of sores is not important to get herpes!! You can get the infection otherwise also, if the partner is infected. The main problem with this virus is that condom does not give 100% protection against it. This is due to the fact that the virus may be in the skin near the genitals, not covered by condom. So, skin to skin contact is another way of spreading this virus!!

### Hepatitis B

Hepatitis B (HBV) is yet another disease which can spread through an infected sexual partner. It is a liver infection caused by Hepatitis B virus. Now, the disease can be acute or chronic. Acute symptoms vanish completely within 6 months of getting infected but once the infection turns chronic, it stays for a pretty long time, or may stay lifelong. The symptoms of Hepatitis B vary widely ranging from a milder form of the disease presenting as weakness, nausea, vomiting, mild fever, sometimes jaundice, pain in your belly, dark coloured urine to as severe as chronic liver disease leading to cancer. Symptoms can last for weeks together. A mere blood test tells us about the infection. The disease is incurable, only treatment is available. Most teens recover within 6 months but your doctor has to keep a close eye on you so that you don't develop chronic infection. Another interesting part is, once you are infected with this virus, you can never donate blood throughout life. So my advice to all teens is to get 3 doses of Hepatitis B vaccine (if not taken earlier).

Sexual contact is one way of spreading this virus. Other ways can be through an infected person's blood, sharing intravenous drug needles, razors or toothbrushes (you simply may not know who is infected!). Get tattoo done at a very good place where they sterilize all instruments.

### Syphilis

Teens are very prone to get this sexually transmitted disease as this is the group having least sexual education and who are desperate to try sex at least once. Unprotected intercourse is the principal mode to get it. You may not have any symptoms but still you can infect many! Actually, there are four stages:

**Stage 1**: A firm and round sore (also called chancre) can be seen in vagina or the area outside vagina or on the skin near anus, lips, hands, penis in males etc. It might not hurt you, so you can simply overlook its presence. Usually, it appears few days or weeks following infection. Treatment is must even if it goes away on its own.

**Stage 2**: If no treatment is taken, you are likely to move to the next phase after a few weeks. Here comes fever, sore throat, skin rashes (more of brown spots on palms, soles, between legs, over the entire body), muscle weakness, hair loss in patches, swollen glands. At times you don't feel like eating anything. The moist areas of the body like the mouth, the area around your private parts or the anus will develop sores or lumps. Now this is the stage when you can spread the infection simply through your rashes WITHOUT sexual contact.

**Stage 3**: No treatment means automatically you are moving to the next stage. Your disease goes to a dormant level, wherein you don't have any symptoms. This stage can last for many years.

**Stage** 4: It is also called Tertiary syphilis. It takes years to reach this stage. This is the most dangerous time when the heart, brain, blood vessels and many other organs are infected and damaged. The stage can end up in death. Otherwise, blindness, heart disease, brain damage, mental illness and paralysis are commonly seen during this phase.

After hearing all this, it is perhaps good to know that this deadly infection can be cured. Your doctor will give you shots of penicillin (or another antibiotic in case you are allergic to the latter). Treatment may follow for a year or so. Please take the complete course and follow your doctor's advice. Do not practice sex while you are on treatment. Once treatment is over, follow up testing becomes mandatory to confirm that you are finally free from this fatal disease.

# Sexual Assault in Adolescents

## About Sexual Assault

An act when someone is touched, kissed, or is penetrated into vagina, mouth or anus forcefully without the person's permission, that is when you have not consented for it. Forcing someone to have sex, even if it does not happen, is also considered an assault. This is very common in teens especially in girls between 14-18 years. About two thirds of the teens would not report about the assault to their parents or, in that sense, to anyone. Sexual abuse or assault can occur in a romantic relationship as well. When in relationship, sometimes you feel pressurized to do something which you really don't want to or at times you are in a situation that you want to say 'NO' but don't know how to, somewhere, you fear that your relation might break and you really don't know how to get out of that situation! This is the time when you are being coerced or emotionally forced to do something you actually don't want to.

The long-term impact of sexual assault can be serious. One of them is the fear that they might be assaulted again! Others can be depression, anxiety, post-traumatic symptoms like how the victim will face her family and society, people will ask her different questions, the person who assaulted her might harm her again, the fright, the agony, and the pain, all contribute to an all-time mental disturbance. This may hamper the physical growth of the adolescent as well. Many victims do not disclose abuse until adulthood. Apart from that, sometimes rape victim might get pregnant or contract certain genital infections which further create a panic situation.

According to a survey, people who commit sexual assault are usually not habitual wrongdoers. Most of them do it for the first time. Many a times these are from the victim's extended family itself or from peer group. Bad touch, trying to kiss the minor or touching her private parts are the commonly attempted acts. Sometimes the victim is small in age and cannot really understand the actions of the perpetrator nor can just oppose to what is going on.

### Evaluation of the Adolescent patient

Evaluation of such a patient needs first to gain her confidence so that she can disclose the entire episode. These minors are not very comfortable or they fear to open up immediately. A good rapport between the care provider (can be a doctor, a nurse or parents) and the victim is really needed so that the teen is able to overcome the barriers and narrate everything. Often the child needs to be taken to a safe and calm place which helps the care provider to extract everything patiently. The provider should be aware of the signs, symptoms and manners suggestive of abuse. Just observe the victim's behaviour during a physical examination, otherwise not revealing much. Try to gain her confidence and discuss treatment with her. The patient may require pain control or may need to be given emergency contraceptive pills in rape cases. Also enquire about commercial sexual exploitation. So, to cut the long story short, bonding between the primary care provider and the victim is more significant than anything else!

Don't make the minor wait for a long time, talk to them very politely, give them time to speak without interrupting; don't just come out with questions. If the child doesn't want to talk now, assure them that you will be there whenever they are ready. Try to stay calm, even if you have strong feelings (anger, guilt etc.) inside. Don't offer them something to eat, drink, and remove clothes or else this may do away with the evidence. If needed, collect the 'unclean' urine sample. If the patient has some injuries then the safety of the child takes precedence over the evidence. If sex was attempted, patient should be evaluated for all sexually transmitted diseases. Mental health of the child should be reviewed and necessary support should be provided to the parents to make this journey easier. A counsellor, who specializes in such cases, can be of immense help. They know the art of extracting things, which in turn helps in reducing the after effects of assault.

Being parents, try to maintain the same routine at home, like going to school, playing with friends, going on outings etc. Do not show much change in the pattern of the usual chores. Or else, the child may think that because of the incident, the environment at home has changed. This makes them more disturbed.

### Yes, Education Works!

Sexual assault is a serious health problem which when addressed appropriately can be prevented to a large extent. If the number of sexual assault cases is to be brought down, education is the best modality for it. Learning programs are the best ways to improve the society. It is high time to mend the thinking of the adolescents. They have to be taught to say 'No', teens should be taught refusal skills, lessons about consent and physical resistance, and onlookers should be empowered to get involved once they see something wrong happening.

Don't allow a person to touch you if it makes you uncomfortable. If someone tries to cross your boundaries or you sense danger, speak your mind and act immediately. Make a scene if necessary. Call the police, and do not think about getting into trouble if you were partying or had drinks at the time of the assault. The most important thing is to talk to someone about what has happened.

Above all, please do not blame yourself for what has happened. The mixed feelings of guilt, anxiety, fear, confusion, shame, that you are getting will not last forever. Don't worry about other people, your health and self-esteem is more important than what others are thinking. This must be a really hard time for you but always remember that your parents and family loves you and will accept you as you are!

# Vaginal Infections in Teens

## Vaginitis in Teens

Vaginitis is nothing but inflammation of the vaginal walls. Inflammation can present itself as any one of the following, or there can be a combination of irritation, swelling, soreness, redness, tenderness, infection. It is caused when normal pH of the vagina is disturbed. When that occurs, there is an imbalance of the normal and harmful bacteria in the vagina, leading to an increase in the concentration of harmful bacteria.

Abnormal vaginal discharge is the most common problem. But before that you should know what is normal vaginal discharge (though I have explained it in detail elsewhere but still let me brief it for you :)). A normal vaginal discharge begins with the onset of puberty especially when breast development is occurring. It is thin, white, not very heavy, not associated with itching and it does not give off that smell. It is due to increase in the levels of hormone oestrogen in your body. Normal vaginal discharge has a tangy or sour aroma, which can be compared to the smell of fermented food. If you get such a smell please do not panic! This is because of the slightly acidic pH of the vagina. Also small shift in your vaginal fragrance is normal because vaginal pH cannot be the same always. There are many things which alter the vaginal pH.

Symptoms of vaginitis can be the following:

+ Colour, amount, consistency and odour of the vaginal discharge changes

+ It can be associated with vaginal itching and soreness

+ It pains when you pee

+ Sex is uncomfortable and hurting

+ There can be an associated minor bleeding or spotting

+ At times you can see rashes especially after intercourse

+ Fever, chills or severe pain in the lowest part of the abdomen are not common.

Vaginitis can be caused by bacteria, yeast, virus or chemicals.

### Yeast Infection

It is mainly caused by fungus candida. It can even occur in pregnancy when there are changes in the hormone levels. Girls with diabetes have more sugar in their urine so they get it often as yeast feeds on sugar. In them, the symptoms may grow worse. They can have bad itching on the opening of the vagina (vestibule), the outer lips (labia majora) and the inner lips (labia minora). Itching is a source of constant irritation, soreness and rashes. Thick white vaginal discharge, resembling cottage cheese, is present. Smell may not be there. Pain at the time of passing urine or during sex may be present.

The main treatment comprises of antifungal powders, creams, vaginal tablets or even the doctor can tell you to take antifungal treatment orally. Sugar intake has to be reduced to a large extent.

## Bacterial Vaginosis

It simply occurs when there is an overgrowth of harmful bacteria in the vagina. It causes a greyish-white, thin vaginal discharge. A fishy odour is typical of bacterial vaginosis. A course of probiotics and antibiotics will help.

## Trichomoniasis

It is caused by a parasite and mainly comes by sexual contact. Very few incidences have shown that it might come by using the same towel or toilet seat or swimming pool earlier used by an infected person. Generally, boys do not have any symptoms and they silently pass the infection to girls during unprotected intercourse. It is revealed only when the girls develop symptoms like greenish-yellow, sometimes frothy discharge, which smells musty (presence of mould like smell) or a pungent fishy odour which is more pronounced than the smell of bacterial vaginosis. There can be painful sex, painful urination, rashes, irritation and soreness. Pain in the lower belly and light bleeding from vagina after sex can be experienced by few. But don't worry, this problem is completely treatable. Oral antibiotics will only help you and your partner.

## Viral Vaginitis

The main culprits are Herpes simplex virus (HSV) and Human papilloma virus (HPV). Both are contracted through sex without the use of your saviours, the condoms! There can be painful sores or warts in the vagina or on the area outside the vagina, including the nearby areas. At times, warts may not be present. You will be treated with antiviral medicines. HPV tends to stay in your body for long. In certain girls, it might lead to cancer of the vulva, vagina or anus later on.

## Non-infectious Vaginitis

Sometimes there is itching, burning, rashes or even discharge without infection. This can be because of irritation or an allergic reaction that occurred from the use of certain detergents, perfumed soaps, fabric softeners, vaginal sprays/deodorants or even with the use of some new brand of sanitary napkins! Tight clothing, at times, contributes to it (especially in hot and humid environment). Simply do away with the cause, keep the area clean, dry and stay hydrated. Steroid cream can be applied if symptoms persist.

## A Forgotten "Tampon"

Yes dear, you heard it right and mind you, its' not only you, many young, pretty girls forget tampon inside the vagina. It is only when there is a rotten odour (like that of a dead organism!!) that the poor tampon is remembered and taken out.

## Important DOs and DON'Ts

+ Talk to paediatrician or gynaecologist, if you notice your child scratching a lot, before surrounding skin becomes raw and open to bacterial infections

+ Pay close attention to onset of any vaginal symptom

+ Note the colour, texture, amount and smell of vaginal discharge

+ Over-the-counter medications are to be avoided as far as possible

+ Do not try to shave, pluck, wax or use hair removal creams to get rid of the hair down there (just in order to give it a cleaner look!) before seeking doctor's advice

+ If you are not in a situation to see the doctor immediately, start probiotics, stay hydrated, avoid sex, do not use nylon, satin or silk panties, avoid tight clothing, preferably use panty liners (change them at least 4-5 times daily), avoid excess sugar and eliminate any vaginal sprays, perfumed soaps or other chemicals used recently

＊ Before visiting the doctor, do not douche with the aim of cleaning the abnormal discharge from the vagina. This way, you are doing more harm by removing the left-over good bacteria

＊ Use breathable cotton undergarments and clothes

＊ Sometimes vaginal infection is associated with urine infection. Let your doctor know if you have burning or pain while passing urine or the frequency of urine has increased

＊ Condoms are the only trusted method to prevent sexually transmitted diseases. Inculcate it in your daily routine, especially those with multiple sexual partners

＊ Do not have intercourse while you are on treatment for vaginitis till the infection is completely wiped off

- Do not use the left over creams or antibiotics or someone else's medications just because the other person had similar complaints! Do not self-medicate

- Young girls should discuss about HPV vaccine with their doctor. Try to take the shots before getting sexually active, any time after 9 years of age

- Try to strengthen your immunity by embracing healthy eating and hygiene habits. Nutritious food, adequate sleep, regular exercise and managing stress play a vital role.

# Depression in Teens- Is It Normal

## Topic Overview

Depression is not uncommon these days, whether you talk about adults or teens. In fact, it has become a serious medical illness, but at the same time, it is treatable. You will see a remarkable change in how a person feels, the way they think and the way they act. There is negativity all around which becomes even worse as time passes. There is a feeling of sadness and/or a loss of interest in activities you once enjoyed. There are major mood swings.

There are no specific medical tests to diagnose teenage depression. Whenever you see your child staying irritated or unhappy most of the times and that is continuing for days together, don't take it lightly, your child might be suffering from depression and needs proper care and management. In teenage, there are hormonal changes which are going on in the body and these further add to the annoyed behaviour. The child may demand to be in isolation, remaining quiet at all times without any reason, may lose interest in various activities, not able to concentrate on majority of things and hesitates to share the matters with family or friends. Eating habits and timings generally change. There may be compulsive overeating or a loss of appetite. They may stay closed in their rooms for hours, may have disturbed sleep or sleep for longer durations. Teenager may experience inappropriate guilt or at times show irresponsible behaviour and may indulge in criminal activities like stealing things. Memory loss, sadness, anxiety, feeling of hopelessness, withdrawal from friends may be few other important and newer developments.

Of course, most teens feel unhappy at times. It is shown by various studies that one out of every eight adolescents has depression. But depression can be completely managed and treated. Only recognising it well in time, understanding your child's mentality at that time, supporting the child, listening to him or her, trying to calmly solve all problems, giving your child company and not leaving them alone should be the target.

Teen depression may not have bigger reasons. Being parents, you may feel that the reasons are quite useless or they are small to grumble over it or they might seem unreal to you but your teen may relate them to his or her self-esteem. The usual reasons might be lower grades in school, or the achievements are not at par with what was expected from them. It may be as simple as their physical appearance or sexual orientation. Again disturbed family life plays a key role.

School grades are an important issue to be sorted. Sometimes parents' constant demand or pressure to excel in all fields makes them more fearful, and in fact weak. This may result from lack of adequate or quality sleep or they feel they don't get enough time to do what they want. They are in fact doing what their parents want them to do. So being parents one should be very cautious before imposing such restrictions or pressurizing them. Good grades are very important but good grades don't guarantee a successful life in future. Let them find happiness in every small thing they do; as long as you feel they are following the right path.

Whatever the children see or listen at home has a great influence on their mental health. Parents are advised to be very clear and careful with the language they use with their children, even with each other. A sense of respect towards each family member is very important. Teenagers expect the same respect which you expect from them. The age is such that they are very vulnerable to any abusive language or harsh words. Shame and punishment can make an adolescent feel worthless and inadequate. Again, decisions regarding their future or studies or any other matter related to them, should be taken jointly, taking the teens into consideration. Making self-decisions or being overprotective can be perceived as a lack of faith in their abilities. This can make them feel less confident. Parents should give space to children especially when they enter their teens. Their views should be respected. Teens should not be forced to do things your way.

Looking good and attractive is something very important for teens. This makes them more confident. Teenage life is such that even pimples, obesity, extremely lean body, good clothes, and all such things matter. They can get depressed very soon when it comes to these things.

When such matters are not sorted out even being with family or friends or doing things which the teen usually enjoys, it directly indicates that the teen is in depression and needs medical help. Health care professionals conduct a series of joint sessions with parents and friends or may interview the teen alone to come to some conclusion. The risk of major damage to oneself or the risk of suicide can only be made out after such sessions. Subsequently, a management protocol is decided. Studies have shown that a combination of antidepressants and psychotherapy play a significant role. Support, from family and teachers, is usually needed. Hospitalization is done only in extreme cases.

# Date Rape Drugs

### Definition

Drugs that make it simpler for someone to rape or sexually assault another person are known as date-rape drugs. Alcohol and other drugs are among them. The individual who has been attacked may become disoriented, have difficulty defending himself or herself, or forget what happened afterwards.

On a date, "date rape" does not necessarily occur. Someone you've just met or someone you've known for a long time could be your attacker. About 2/3rd of the rapes are committed by a known person. This means that the vast majority of women are raped by men that they know, whether they are friends, people they are dating, co-workers, acquaintances, or even family members. Therefore, be very careful.

### Common Types of Date-Rape Drugs

There are many kinds of drugs to overpower someone or cause them to forget an incident. The most common date-rape drugs are:

**GHB (gamma-hydroxybutyric acid):** Actually, Gamma hydroxybutyrate (GHB) is a chemical found in the brain and other areas of the body. It can also be made in a laboratory in a liquid form or as a powder. Neither of the two has a smell or a taste. At times, this drug is used by doctors for treating excessive daytime sleepiness which is also known as narcolepsy. Taking GHB seems to reduce symptoms occurring as a result of withdrawal of alcohol, heroin, morphine, and other opioid drugs, thereby preventing relapse.

Now what happens when it is consumed by the victim?

It can cause hallucinations, confusion, memory loss, a slowed heart rate, slowed breathing, fits, coma, and even death. Long-term use can lead to addiction and withdrawal symptoms when it is stopped.

Taking GHB along with alcohol may greatly increase this effect.

This is a depressant that has many nicknames: easy lay, Georgia home boy, liquid X, liquid ecstasy, liquid E, or fantasy.

**Rohypnol (flunitrazepam):** This drug belongs to a class of depressants called benzodiazepines. It works by dramatically slowing the function of the central nervous system. It causes deep sleep and makes the victim debilitated making him/her easy prey. For recreational activities or in clubs, it is taken along with alcohol. The other common names are circles, forget pill, forget-me-pill, la rocha, lunch money drug, Mexican valium, rope, and many more. It, sometimes, is prescribed as a short-term treatment when it is hard to fall asleep or given to help relax someone prior to receiving anaesthesia. Again, this too has no flavour and dissolves easily in liquids. You can't make out the drug in dark- coloured drinks but, yes, in a light-coloured beverage, Rohypnol will dye the drink blue. So BEWARE guys!

So, what do you feel when you take it?

As an immediate effect, there is going to be kind of, feeling pukish, feeling too hot and too cold at the same time, feeling faint or very weak, there can be complete confusion, disorientation, which appears within 10 minutes of ingestion. You might struggle to speak and move, become socially constrained, and suffer from vision difficulties, you are unable to empty all the urine from your bladder and the list goes on. It can even lead to complete black outs. The majority of people who use the drug have no recollection of what happened while they were using it.

**Ketamine:** The usual indication for using Ketamine is to put you to sleep before surgery and to prevent pain and discomfort during certain medical tests or procedures. Sometimes, it is used for patients with depression. Now this, once again, may be used as a date rape drug. Ketamine is a clear liquid or an off-white powder that's frequently injected. It has no smell or taste. Its nicknames include Special K, vitamin K, and cat Valium. It makes you feel far from reality. It can also cause an upset stomach, vomiting, high blood pressure, changes in your heart rate, seizures, or a coma. Its effect usually occurs within 30 minutes and lasts 1-2 hours.

**Alcohol:** The above drugs when used with alcohol potentiate its effects. But alcohol in itself can render a person incapable to defend himself or herself. Person may be confused later, finding it difficult to remember what exactly has happened.

### A Personal Advice!!

Dear Girls, there are a few safety measures which can be kept in mind while you are partying or in a gathering. Try to go out with your besties, whom you trust. Wherever you go, leave the place with that group of friends only. Inform someone at home that you are going somewhere and the probable time of returning back. If possible, give the complete address of the place you are going to visit.

Let someone know who all will be there in the party (if you know tentatively). Know that, if your gut tells you the situation is not okay, you should leave the gathering as soon and as safely as you can. Keep your alcohol intake under control. Do not accept drinks from strangers. Anything that tastes weird should be avoided. Never leave your drink unattended. If you left one, try and get a new one.

Sometimes, the party has a loud music, so in that case if you wish to go to the restroom, let a friend accompany you. Let other friends also know where you are going. Undue attention from anyone should raise the alarm in you. Unwanted touch should be bravely opposed.

In case you are actually going on a date and do not want to disclose it, try choosing a restaurant, a park or any other public place initially. Do not opt for visiting the person's house or a friend's place or any other isolated location. Do not accept any drink or eatables from the other person when at a remote place.

If you are entering a college, you should be aware of the fact that the majority of the rapes happen during the first few weeks of the year. This is the time when students tend to make new friends, getting closer to certain people. Always stick with your friends and your sound judgement.

Last but not the least, always keep your phone charged.

# Birth Control Methods for Teens

Although hard to believe but most teens are sexually active these days with exception of very few. Sorry to say, but that too, unprotected sex without any concern about the consequences! Limited knowledge regarding the safety methods drives them either towards unplanned pregnancy or sexually transmitted diseases. There are many options available for protection, the easiest and simplest being the condom.

There are other methods also, of which hormonal methods are the most widely used. But the hormonal methods are not recommended for those who have had blood clots, liver problems, or migraine headaches.

Those who have had unexplained vaginal bleeding (bleeding that is not during their periods) or who think they may be pregnant or carry the fear of getting a sexually transmitted disease should talk to their doctor.

Almost all hormonal methods have similar ways of functioning. There is a slow release of hormone/hormones in the body, which prevent the release of the egg from the ovary. Once the egg is not released, the sperm will not have anything to fertilize. The other way is by making the secretions of the cervix (opening of the uterus inside the vagina) thicker, so that the sperm is unable to reach the tube and fertilize the egg. It hinders the sperm from travelling up the reproductive tract. But they have no effect on sexually transmitted diseases (STDs).

So, let's talk about the various methods in detail:

### Implant

Implant is a small, flexible plastic tube that will be put under the skin of your upper arm. The tube releases the hormone progestin, which can help protect against pregnancy for up to 3 years. But it has no protection from sexually transmitted diseases! No daily care is needed.

## Intrauterine Device (IUD)

Yes, you heard it right. It is a small T-shaped plastic device which is inserted in the uterus. Two types of IUDs are available: one is covered with copper and the other releases the hormone progestin.

The effect of the copper lasts up to 10 years. Progestin IUDs can work for 3 to 6 years, depending on the brand. The IUD does not protect against STDs.

## Injection (Shot)

It is another effective way to get rid of an unwanted pregnancy. The shot is given after every 3 months, which means the hormone, progestin, will remain in your body for 3 months. Couples having sex using this method must wear a condom in order to protect themselves against STDs.

## Birth Control Pill

The 'Pill' is a daily pill which has to be taken at a particular time each day. The pill contains either one hormone or a combination of two hormones but the action remains more or less the same (as described above).

The pack contains either 21 pills (to be continued for 21 days) or 24 pills (to be continued for 24 days). After this, there has to be a pill free period of either 7 days or 4 days, respectively, depending on which pill was taken. A new pack is then started after the gap.

There is another kind of pill, which is an emergency pill. Now, this pill is to be taken as soon as possible after each intercourse, preferably within the first 72 hours of unprotected sex. Again, you are at risk of getting sexually transmitted diseases.

## Birth control Patch

The birth control patch is a thin, beige, 1¾-inch (4½-centimeter) square patch that sticks to the skin. It releases hormones through the skin into the bloodstream to prevent pregnancy. You will put the patch on the first day of your period, change it once a week for 3 weeks in a row. The patch should be applied either on the abdomen or buttocks or upper outer arm, or upper body - except for the breasts. On the fourth week, no patch is worn, and your chums should start during this time.

Next time, the patch is applied at a different location from the previous one. Bathing, swimming or exercising does not have an impact on the action of the patch nor the patch gets removed so easily. If the patch falls off by any chance, apply a replacement patch.

## Ring

The birth control ring is a flexible circular device that goes inside the vagina. It slowly releases hormones through the vaginal wall into the bloodstream, thereby preventing pregnancy. The Ring is to be put inside the vagina on Day 1 of your cycle, where it stays for 3 weeks at a stretch and is taken out on the last day of the third week. Even being inside the vagina, it will not save you from sexual diseases so better use a condom with it. But on the other hand, few girls might experience vaginal irritation and increased amount of vaginal discharge along with other side effects.

## Condom

Condoms are nothing but thin pouches that keep the girls away from sperms. There are male condoms as well as female condoms.

## Male condom

It is to be worn on penis each time before attempting sex. At the end of the intercourse, the male secretions collect into this pouch. It is then safely removed from penis and discarded in the prescribed manner.

## Female Condom

Condom for female has rings on both the sides. The ring on the closed side is to be gently inserted inside the vagina and taken as deep as possible. Let the outer ring hang about an inch outside the vagina. The female condom can be worn eight hours before the intercourse but should be removed immediately after sex, before getting up from the bed.

DO NOT use male and female condoms at the same time as friction can break them. Also, a condom cannot be reused.

Now these condoms help protect from sexually transmitted diseases. But in case infection is on any part of the skin which is not covered by condom, that infection can be easily carried.

## Diaphragm

A diaphragm is a dome-shaped bowl made of thin, flexible silicone that sits over the cervix, so that the sperms can't get in and fertilize an egg. The diaphragm can be put in up to 2 hours before having sex, and must be left in place for at least 6 hours after sex. The diaphragm should not stay in longer than 24 hours. Again it does not protect against STDs.

## Spermicide

A spermicide is basically a chemical to stop the sperms from going up to the egg. They can be in the form of cream, gel, foam, film or suppository. A spermicide has to be put in the vagina minimum 15 minutes before intercourse, so that it has time to dissolve and spread. But these are not very effective in controlling pregnancy. So be careful!

## Fertility Awareness Methods

In simple words, do not have sex around the time of ovulation (when the ovary releases the egg) or use a reliable birth control method at that time. The trick is to know your ovulation time. In a regular 28 days cycle, ovulation generally occurs 14 days prior to the next menses, so roughly around the 14$^{th}$ day of the cycle. But please girls do not go by this rule as you never know when your next periods are going to start! Some people go by ovulation kits, others, by the thickness of their vaginal discharge and so on.

There is another rough way of estimation. Leave the first and last 10 days of your cycle. Use condoms or other reliable methods in the middle 8-10 days of the menstrual cycle to avoid pregnancy. Now this applies only if you get regular monthly cycles on the same date (+/- 2-3 days).

Also note that there is no fixed time of ovulation in PCOD patients rather I would say many cycles might go without ovulation. So always use protection and please do not think that you have PCOD and you will not get pregnant!!

## Withdrawal

Withdrawal, also called pulling out, is when a male removes his penis from the vagina before he ejaculates during sex. This is not an effective method to control pregnancy as sperms might leak into the vagina even before ejaculation. This method should not be used especially around the time of ovulation as there are high chances of failure.

**Side effects with hormonal methods**

Some of the common side effects with the hormonal methods:

- Irregular periods or no periods

- Heavier or lighter periods

- Spotting between periods

- Weight gain, headache, acne, nausea, breast tenderness

- Depression

- Mood swings

# Injuries in Adolescents

**Injuries – Why are adolescents at risk?**

Injuries pose a particular threat to adolescents. Teens get amused and entertained when they engage in risk-taking and sensation seeking behaviours. This is more common with boys especially. I sometimes feel that there is a lack of adult supervision and personal attention due to increased developmental and social factors. Due to a lot of work pressure and fulfilment of commitments, somewhere the teen's activities go unnoticed. Hormonal changes and a lack of knowledge of the various consequences are other factors which play a part. Peer initiation and a lack of skills to resist peer pressure are frequently seen.

### Common causes of Adolescent Injuries

Road traffic injuries and drowning are the leading causes of death among adolescents worldwide. These deaths are largely predictable and preventable. Teens are generally crazy for motor vehicle use, and the manner in which they drive the vehicle is completely different from an adult driving. They tend to violate the traffic rules and indulge in overspeeding, use of mobile phones while driving, driving under the influence of alcohol and dangerous overtaking. They forget that they are totally inexperienced. Actually, this is a stage where the influence of parents is reduced and adolescents want to take control of their lives.

Drowning is again common among teenagers. Males are especially at risk of drowning due to increased exposure to water and riskier behaviours such as swimming alone, drinking alcohol before swimming alone and boating.

Not only the youngsters but the authorities also sometimes lack in their job. Yet, despite the alarming statistics, road and water safety for children and adolescents is often overlooked in public health policies. Also, the pre hospital first aid and early evacuation from the accident site are often unheeded.

Violence is another key factor leading to injuries in teens. Violence comes from aggression. A child never learns violence in one day. If aggressive behaviour is not mended timely, some day it will turn into violence. A violent teen can cut or pierce his/her soft tissues by instruments such as knives, power hand tools, and household appliances. Not only at home, the adolescent tries to use violence to exert social control over others and to resolve interpersonal conflicts. Here, parents and teachers should take the lead. Try to nip the evil in the bud and teach the teens how to cope with it. We should help adolescents achieve healthy independence and become productive members of society.

There can be other unintentional injuries like poisonings, burns, and fall from a higher level. Playing sports is yet another very common reason of injury. There can be non-sports injuries: at home, at school while simply playing, at other public places. While most injuries can be managed outside hospital environment, but there are certain injuries for which medical aid becomes necessary.

## Adolescent Sports Injuries

Passion for sports is very common in teens. And why shouldn't it be! Sports should form a vital part of their daily curriculum. Sports like football, basketball, hockey, softball, baseball, track and field sports are commonly practised. These are quite likely to end up with minor scrapes and bruises. Sometimes injury can be major. Physical injuries can affect the tendons, ligaments, bones, and/or muscles. Pain and swellings can be caused due to injuries to the knees, shoulders, elbow, back, and heel. Prompt medical aid can save from complications. Very common among them are overuse injuries, over training and burn out.

## Overuse injuries

These tend to happen when too much stress is being laid on any part of the body. Same movements are being repeated again and again, which eventually result in pain, swelling, strain in the muscle and tissue damage. Areas most affected by overuse injuries are the elbows, shoulders, knees, and heels. Not only do sports lead to such injuries, even playing a certain musical instrument repeatedly is regarded as overuse of certain hand or arm movements. Teens are more prone to such injuries owing to their growth spurts. Sitting in front of computers for long can even produce the same results.

The symptoms which ensue are tingling, numbness, pain, stiffness, soreness, weakness and fatigue. Overuse injuries tend to get worse without medical aid. So, seek the doctor timely and avoid missing your favourite sport!

### Overtraining

Teens should clearly know the demarcation between training and overdoing. And here coaches have a big role to play. Training should be clearly monitored and supervised. Overtraining will make the adolescent exhaust very soon. He/she will not have the strength to do the actual training. With increased intensity of training, there is hardly any time for recovery. The injuries mostly involve the muscles, joints and ligaments. Not only the teen experiences a feeling of increased difficulty and fatigue throughout the day, abnormal muscle soreness and pain, there will also be disturbed sleep, decreased motivation and altered concentration. Strength and endurance will be decreased with impaired motion and coordination.

Rest is a big healer. It will enable the body to be fully prepared for the next workout.

## Burnout

A stage of burnout comes when the adolescent is performing the same repetitions and intensity of sports everyday but still there is declining performance. These teens are easily fatigued and lack motivation. They are actually in a state of chronic stress. They no longer enjoy the activity which they earlier used to appreciate and adore. Burnout is not an overnight process. It is gradual and subtle at first but later on gets worse.

So, lets' abide by the common proverb, "Prevention is better than cure". Be sensible about the amount of time you spend on each movement. Exercise regularly and stay active as it will increase your overall flexibility and strength.

If certain injury is ignored at any point of time, it can turn into lifelong pain. Adolescence is a growing stage, so injuries during this time can adversely affect the growth of a bone or a soft tissue. They will become more prone for fractures later in life.

# Violence in Teens

## Teen Violence

It is the deliberate and planned use of physical force or power by teens, to bully or harm someone. It can range from simple threats to fighting, with or without the use of weapons, sometimes even leading to death. Violent acts not only cause physical harm but can have a great emotional impact as well.

Violence in teens does not pop up suddenly. It needs to have some basis for violence to erupt in the adolescent age group. They may have seen someone at school and been tempted to it. But many times it is inherited from one's own family or parents! What they see at home influences them more than anything else. Teens between the ages of 14-18 years are more vulnerable to get involved in one or the other type of violent behaviour as in hitting someone, slapping, bullying, sexual or dating violence.

Generally, teens who get involved in violent acts experience several health conditions or possess certain risk behaviours as in missing school, not doing well in studies, they are kind of indulged in substance use (alcohol, drugs, tobacco), are not content with something or the other, feel sad and hopeless, are involved in risky sexual behaviour, sometimes they love to carry weapons with them (may be just a simple knife!). Many a times their physical appearance, obesity or extreme slimness, makes them violent. Numerous such incidences have come up wherein the parents, due to their economic and monetary conditions, are not able to buy or provide the teen with what they have seen with their friends. This makes the teen feel dissatisfied over petty things, eventually leading them to adopt violent manners.

### How to make teens "Gentle and Kind"

Just teach them to make healthy choices because the teen's brain is still growing. Sit with them and make them understand the difference between good and bad. You can speak about the consequences of violent acts, how they can ruin a person's life if they indulge in one. Studies will suffer, personal life will get disturbed, they may be forced to leave school, and overall, their future will be at stake. They may face various health issues in adulthood. They may get injured and become disabled, leaving a lifelong impact on their psychology and social functioning. Not only the adolescent will suffer, but it distresses the entire family.

Poor monitoring and a lack of supervision by parents may contribute to teen violence. Parents should adopt consistent disciplinary practices at home. Do not be too harsh or too lax with them. If there is unemployment in the family or you are facing depression, do not reveal your failures in front of your children. They may get demoralised. Try to keep the children away from it as far as possible.

Get involved in their day-to-day activities. Find out their association with some criminal minded peers and/or gang membership. Teens normally may not be aggressive but they find themselves powered in groups and this is the time when they give way to risk taking behaviours.

Arguments are a part of every household but always mark your words, especially when youngsters are around. Children learn by example, so if they see violence at home, they will definitely follow it when they grow up. Please reconsider your parenting styles or join some good parenting workshops. Don't be reluctant to seek help and don't be ashamed of being judged as a bad parent. You should understand that your aggression and violence are affecting not only you but your kid's mentality too.

Any conflicts with friends should be resolved early. Prolonged fights with friends may make the teens frustrated and depressed. Try to find out the root cause of their anger. Your child may be struggling with how to manage his/her feelings. Simply ignoring such behaviour won't help it go away. Give them space. Be patient and listen to them. Give them confidence and let them develop self-strategies to cope up with the situation.

Teens should not have easy access to alcohol, tobacco or cigarettes. These substances make the adolescents feel good in the beginning, but later, when they don't get an adequate amount, they become violent.

Studies have shown that violence in the media also impacts teens. Playing violent video games intensifies aggressive feelings and actions in teens. Indirect health effects can include an increase in heart rate and increase in blood pressure. Not only video games, internet, television, movies, all can contribute. Here comes the role of stern supervision. Please check and verify the content before allowing your teens to watch. In short, positive parenting skills are very important. Teens should have consistent interaction with and direction from their parents.

Teens that are identified as gay, lesbian, bisexual or not sure of their sexual identity are more likely to experience violence than their heterosexual peers. Schools can adopt policies and practices to create safe and supportive environments for all young people. Sooner or later, society has to accept such teens if violence is to be reduced.

There is something called Post-traumatic stress disorder (PTSD). If the teen has lost someone very dear, may it be a friend or someone very close, their anger may come out as a normal emotion, but if they get violent, that needs to be addressed. They need your constant support at that time. Counselling, here, becomes a necessary measure.

If teens are mentally not well as in bipolar disorder, attention-deficit hyperactivity disorder (ADHD) or they fall prey to autism, they tend to develop a violent approach. A very mild attitude towards them, repeated sittings with the psychologist and the prescribed medications go a long way towards helping them. Assistance should be sought from teachers and school friends. It should be understood that these teens are violent owing to their illness and not otherwise. Self - harming is another added fear.

Nowadays, there are many social developmental programmes, specifically tailored and aimed to help the children manage their anger. These programmes should become part of the school curriculum.

# Substance Use in Teens

*What do you mean by "Substance"?*

*A Substance is anything that, when consumed, has mood altering qualities, or that might cause significant problems or distress. The substance in that case might be alcohol, tobacco, marijuana and other riskier drugs. The problems which the adolescent may face is feeling dizzy, weak, and unconscious, missing routine activities; driving a vehicle in such a scenario is even more unsafe. Dependence on any substance is determined, to a large extent, by culture and society where the teen is growing. There are other issues like genetic factor, environmental stress, psychiatric problems, social pressure or let me say, peer pressure. Experimentation with alcohol and drugs during adolescence is common. Unfortunately, teenagers often don't see the* link between their actions today and the consequences tomorrow. It is very difficult to predict which teens will stop consuming, who will become occasional drinkers, and who will be addicts.

### Risks of Substance Use

Substance use tends to affect your teen's growth and development, especially brain development, wherein it damages the various connections in the brain. These teens have a reduced ability to experience pleasure. It also creates problems with memory. Puberty might be delayed, and it has a bad effect on the reproductive system. The bones tend to get weaker, making limbs shorter with reduced growth.

Such adolescents are not too far from attempting risky behaviours such as unprotected sex or driving a vehicle at high speed. Even as adults, they may contract diseases like heart problems, diabetes, high levels of bad cholesterol, sleep disorders and liver problems. Very soon, this substance "use" gets converted into substance "abuse". The earlier in life teens start using these substances, the greater the chance of them become addicted to it. Over a period of time, they look weak, exhausted, older than their age, often with red eyes, lasting cough, they are least concerned about hygiene and by that time many other health issues might be on the go. Depression and anxiety may ensue shortly. They might have sudden mood swings, become irritable, start arguments, break rules and withdraw from the family. Their interest in school decreases over time, and they develop a negative attitude and discipline problems.

A major point of fear comes, when over time, these teens develop tolerance or the need to use more drugs or alcohol to get the same affect. And when they don't consume these, they get withdrawal symptoms. In other words, they develop an alcohol dependency. Sometimes, the teens may develop suicidal behaviour.

Over time some teens might be involved in criminal activities. They may not get sufficient money to fulfil their needs, so they may opt for stealing etc. Driving a vehicle at a high speed gives them immense pleasure, leading to road accidents. Unprotected sex might lead to sexually transmitted diseases including HIV. Unplanned pregnancies are not too far in the list. They become academically weak losing multiple career opportunities. The relationships with family and friends suffer to a great extent.

## Now what can be done?

Parents play a crucial role in the lives of their children. A child may not learn what you say but yes, they definitely learn what their parents do. So, if you want your child to stay away from any particular substance, try not to consume it in front of your children. For them, it then becomes a normal affair. If you drink, do so in moderation. Teens should not have easy access to alcohol or cigarettes. Just talk to them about various substances, try to tell the harmful effects, and be open to them. Try to become their role models, teach them responsible behaviour. When they become teens, treat them more like friends, listen to them, talk about their friends, and try to eliminate any such peer you think might instil bad habits in your child. Try to recognise their problems and help them make healthy choices. A single such conversation is not going to be helpful. You may require multiple conversations at regular intervals but please avoid lectures! Such conversations should be short, making sense of your words. Assure your teen that he or she can be honest with you. You can emphasize how substance use can affect things that are important to your teen like sports, appearance, holidays, etc.

It is very important to discuss with them the ways to resist peer pressure. Teach them to say 'NO' to substance use. Make them strong from the inside, only then they will be able to turn down such offers. At times, parents consume alcohol or cigarettes. In such cases, try to explain what you feel after consuming, what changes you have observed in yourself over time, how your health has changed and how difficult it is to completely abandon the habit.

Pay attention to your teen's whereabouts. Make certain family rules such as setting a particular time before which the child should be at home. After returning home, try to extract things calmly. Do not forget to praise even after a minor achievement. Encouragement is a big booster.

Prescription pain killers, cough syrups and other medicines should be kept secure and closely monitored. Any prescription medications that are no longer being used should not remain in the home. If you think your teen is involved in significant drug use, contact a doctor, counsellor or other health care provider for help.

# HIV/AIDS in Teens

## Overview

Human immunodeficiency virus (HIV) attacks the immune system rendering it weak, thereby reducing the body's ability to fight off infections and some kinds of cancer. AIDS is a more severe form of HIV which comes after many years of acquiring HIV.

Adolescents and youngsters contribute a major chunk to total HIV patients worldwide. Adolescent HIV should be regarded as a separate entity from adult HIV as the teens face much more teething troubles as compared to adults. HIV in teens is a real stigma wherein there is fear about their future, their education, their growing health needs and lifelong treatment. A most important concern is their marriage, as this disease will remain with them throughout their lives. Adolescence is actually an age of transformation from childhood to much more mature beings. And HIV/AIDS during this time will make this transformation even more challenging. This is the age when the child has just learned to understand his/her body, and on top of this, the symptoms of HIV infection make life even more chaotic.

## Who are at more risk of contracting HIV/AIDS?

HIV spreads when infected blood or body fluids (such as semen or vaginal fluids) enter the body. HIV is not spread through saliva, tears, sweat, urine, touching, hugging, shaking hands, sharing dishes, "social kissing" etc. Among the various risk factors and situations leading to adolescent HIV are adolescent sex workers, child trafficking, child labour, childhood sexual abuse and coercive sex with an older person. Another common mode of HIV transmission is from mother to child during pregnancy, delivery or breastfeeding. The teens involved in drugs and other substance abuse may acquire it directly through used and infected needles. Also, under the influence of alcohol or other drugs, the adolescents may indulge in risky behaviours and go in for sex without condom. Lack of awareness of contraception, especially from where to obtain it, is the key lacuna leading to unprotected intercourse. Another common cause of acquiring HIV is the high rates of sexually transmitted diseases (STDs) among youth. An STD increases the risk of getting or spreading HIV.

Tattooing or body piercing can lead to HIV infection only if the equipment or ink has someone else's blood in it. This is more likely to happen when unsterilized needles or ink are used.

## Difficulties faced in the management of Adolescents

Emotional trauma in these teens is very difficult to handle. Most of them have never even heard of the disease. Many teens may blame their mothers or parents for giving them the infection during delivery or afterwards. They may not be so confident in their behaviour since they take it as a social stigma. It may hamper their education. Clinically, the HIV infected adolescents present as physically stunted individuals, with delayed puberty and adrenarche. Mental illness and substance abuse are important comorbidities. These teens require proper and appropriate counselling. Another big issue with these children is their adherence to medicines. Since they are too small to understand the depth of the problem, so being particular for treatment schedule is a bit challenging for them. At times they are ashamed and guilty of their HIV status, so they may hide their medicines from others and tend to skip the doses. Many adolescents with HIV do not even know they are HIV positive.

Child's growth and development is another aspect which cannot be overlooked. The dose of medicines in HIV children and teens depend not on their age but on their weight. With increasing growth, there is constant change in weight so regular follow ups with the doctor become a must in them. Side effects of HIV medicines are harsh to bear especially for those children who have just entered their teens. Cost of the treatment is an additional burden particularly when it is not covered by insurance.

# Adolescent Pregnancy

## Overview

Pregnancy occurring before the age of 20 years (between 13-19 years) is an adolescent pregnancy. Adolescent pregnancy is a global issue. It was a normal affair in previous centuries, but now the rates are constantly declining, especially in developed countries. It mainly occurs in underdeveloped nations, where it is commonly driven by poverty and lack of education. At times, girls are pressurized to marry early and bear children. Adolescents who may want to avoid pregnancies may not be able to do so due to knowledge gaps and misconceptions on where to obtain contraceptive methods and how to use them. At many places in the world, sexual violence is a major issue. This again contributes to teenage pregnancy. Many a times the pregnancy is unplanned and just occurs.

Another common problem in many adolescents is irregular menstrual cycles, because of which judgement cannot be made regarding the ovulation time and pregnancy ensues. These girls are incidentally found to be pregnant when they approach the doctor for missed periods. By that time, they are already 3 or 4 months pregnant.

## Health Consequences

Very early pregnancy, as in the teens is a major cause of maternal death worldwide. The major chunk of it is contributed by the low and middle income countries. Due to a lack of awareness, these girls may opt for unsafe abortion practices and land up in severe infections, sometimes leading to death. In case they continue their pregnancies, the other issues with them can be high blood pressure, fits in pregnancy, anaemia, heavy bleeding after delivery, premature birth etc. These girls may not get pregnancy care from the very beginning so they land up in various difficulties.

A baby born before time has to be kept in Infant's ICU (intensive care unit) for further care. These babies will be of low birth weight and can get severe infections due to poor immune system. As a result, they need to be kept in ICU for many days.

## Social Consequences

Unmarried, pregnant teenage girls might face stigma or violence from family and peers. They may not be socially accepted. This is another cause of school dropout, indirectly affecting the educational status and income potential of the family. Pregnancies occurring before 15 years of age have irreparable consequences in terms of the violation of the rights of girls and life-threatening concerns related to sexual and reproductive health. The risk of death during or after delivery is higher in these girls.

## How to manage an Adolescent Pregnancy

Pregnant adolescents face almost the same issues in pregnancy as faced by other mature women. But if pregnancy occurs before 15 years of age, the body is still not physically developed to sustain a healthy pregnancy or to give birth. Teens should get pregnancy care from the very beginning. Awareness should be given about the various contraceptives or they should at least know the early symptoms of pregnancy so that there is no delay in approaching the doctor. All blood tests and other investigations should be done timely. Regular check-ups by the doctor are a must. Routine medicines should be consumed as and when prescribed. Adequate diet and nutrition are the basis to deliver a healthy baby. Avoid smoking, alcohol and other drugs in pregnancy.

A holistic approach is needed to address the issues leading to adolescent pregnancy in depth. The issues such as poverty, social pressure, gender inequality, forced sex and lower educational levels are the mainstay in eradicating the very concept of adolescent pregnancy. It is of utmost importance to impart complete knowledge about the various methods of contraception and these girls should have easy access to these. Even after sexual violence (sexual abuse or rape), immediate contraception should be provided so as to avoid pregnancy as far as possible. Some girls simply get pregnant immediately after marriage out of curiosity or experimentation. In others, there is a family history of teenage pregnancy. Substance abuse is another factor leading to early pregnancy. Safe abortion practice and post abortion care should be followed in all underdeveloped countries.

# Rights of Adolescents

Rights of adolescents vary from country to country and from one region of the world to another. I will be talking about rights in general without targeting any particular religion or nationality. These rights are the most indispensable ones, influencing the very existence of any human being.

### A Teenager's Rights - The basic ones

Once the children enter adolescence, they start to form their identities and need more independence. A sweet home, nutritious food, basic clothing, I think, are the elementary things which every child deserves and should get. Apart from that loving family, primary health care and the right to formal education are the other few.

The teen deserves all the respect in the family. They should be treated as human beings by family and friends. A teen also has the right to be loved. Teens need someone around to provide them with constant support and to listen to them. At this age, it is very important to share your views with them, pay attention to what they have to say. Parents' decisions should not be imposed on them. Rather they should be made a part of it. It is very important for their mental health. They should be shown the right direction. The choices the teens make - or are forced to make - determine their lives now and their future as adults. So be very cautious and patient towards them.

But parents have the right to set rules and limit privileges. Teens should also not take their parents for granted. Parents are parents and they have all rights to say 'NO' when it is actually needed.

Privacy is another sensitive issue, when it comes to teenagers. This has to be handled very delicately. At this stage, parents should behave more like friends and advisors, rather than being strict and rude to them.

Though adolescents have a complete right to education, but parents too, have the full right to monitor their access to the outside world. This generation is more connected through technology, media and the internet than any other generation in human history. Teens should not take advantage of their right to education. Freedom of speech should be given to teens. Parents should try to mould their children's decisions in an encouraging way. Be careful not to embarrass them around their peers.

## Rights of adolescents - To let them live in the society

Adolescents should not be abandoned. They should not be left to fend for themselves on the streets. They have the right to live with dignity. They should be protected from all sorts of violence. The teen years are such that they should not be neglected at any point of time or else they might fall prey to physical or sexual abuse. They have the right to be protected from dangerous drugs. Adequate knowledge should be provided regarding the same.

Apart from that they should have the right to freedom of opinion and expression. Teens should be informed and they should have the right to participate in any decision making that involves them directly or indirectly.

Right to complete their education is another fundamental right, especially for girls. Girls and women are the building blocks of any family or rather I should say, any country! Their education can impact the family for generations. They should learn, relax and play. They have the right to all forms of development - emotional, mental and physical. Girl education in some way can prevent an early marriage and early child bearing.

All adolescents should have rights to make informed choices over their own bodies. Sexual and reproductive health is the cornerstone of the transition from childhood to adolescent group. A number of issues need to be addressed during this transition. Sexual and reproductive health services should be accessible to all adolescents and the services must be responsive, respectful, confidential and affordable. Aims should be to prevent early and/or unintended pregnancies, unsafe abortions, unsafe sexual behaviours, imparting knowledge about HIV and other sexually transmitted diseases, female genital mutilation and gender based violence.

Legal rights of teens are different in each country, so be sure to check with your local authorities.

Many teens are not able to enjoy all the above privileges. Poverty, race, ethnicity, gender and cultural traditions are among the many factors that may stand in the way.